Sparty Lea

An Upland Leadmining Community

Jennifer W. Norderhaug

Sparty Lea

An Upland Leadmining Community

© Jennifer W. Norderhaug

First published 1988

This edition first published November 2008
by
Wagtail Press,
Gairshield,
Whitley Chapel,
Hexham,
Northumberland
NE47 0HS
www.wagtailpress.co.uk

Wagtail Press

Edited by Hilary Kristensen

ISBN: 978-0-9538443-2-6

Designed by T.W.Kristensen

Printed by Robson Print, Hexham

Contents

Introduction

Exactly 20 years ago Joan Ridley of Allenheads encouraged me to publish my diverse collection of Sparty Lea information because, she said, it concerned so many local families, houses and farms. Willie Parker of Sparty Lea helped me make sense of the diaries, ledgers, stories and photographs kindly loaned by local people. This was the very first time that such treasures had been shared outside of their families.The result was a home spun book sold from my home at the old St. Peter's School. It found its way across the globe from America to Australia to people with a Sparty Lea connection. The letters which accompanied the orders were filled with fond memories of life in upper East Allendale – Joan and Willie had been right.

Twenty years later many of the characters mentioned in the original book have passed away and Sparty Lea is now home to some new people who may have come to love the place as I did. I am sure they would like to know about the families who contributed towards the history of this special place.

With the expertise of Wagtail Press "Sparty Lea, an Upland Leadmining Community" has been reborn with much of the original information and some new additions. I hope a new readership will reap as much pleasure as I have done from being acquainted with Sparty Lea. Past and present walk hand in hand here, there is a story to tell around every corner.

Let me take you back in the following pages to 1988 and far beyond ....

J. N. 2008

Sparty Lea (1988)

"Too barren."

"The wildness becomes magnetic."

These were the opinions of two friends of mine on visiting Sparty Lea.

I must say I lean towards the latter view. At 1,000ft, on the edge of the Northern Pennines, with hill farms pushing the peaty moorland higher up the fellside and sturdy stone farm steadings dotted here and there, Sparty Lea has a charismatic touch. A strong atmosphere of the past. Lifestyles long vanished echo along the East Allen Valley and round the huge corner stones of ruined and renovated homes. Even the loneliest, most isolated houses standing aloof and proud on the edge of the moor have a tale to tell, a whole history of their own.

Sparty Lea nestles under the shadow of Killhope Law (just over 2,000ft) in the High Forest grieveship of the East Allen Valley. Sixteen miles south of Hexham, ten miles east of Alston and five miles north of Wearhead, it is almost the last outpost of the south-west corner of Northumberland. Within minutes one reaches the Cumbrian and Durham border posts.

The 30-odd houses are scattered along the valley from the river up into the hillsides over a distance of a mile or so.

The small Post Office remains in business; the Chapel is active; the nearest Women's Institute and Carpet Bowls Club, held in the next village of Allenheads (the highest village in England), comprise members mainly from Sparty Lea. Traders sell their goods by van - coal, milk, fish and meat - and the nearest Co-op, six miles down the valley in Allendale, delivers orders once a week.

There is a daily bus service, except Sunday; the County Library van trundles from farm to cottage, and Swaledale sheep, cows and bulls pull peacefully at the upland grasses. The name itself is derived from the meadows with tough reed grasses or sparts.

Lead mining breathed life into the area and sustained its people for over 200 years. In the 18th and 19th centuries Sparty Lea was a buzzing hive of activity with three lead mines in fewer miles. The Blackett Beaumont family were the owners, and the lives of the busy, mainly Methodist, dales community centred around the mines, the chapels, the church, the school, local fairs and shows, and farming.

Most miners had a few acres attached to their cottages and kept pigs, a cow and hens to supplement their income. Fuel was cut locally and many would be the evening where neighbours visited and chatted over the peaty, glowing hearth. They made their own entertainment and, although there's no denying times would be hard, there was always a deep community involvement. Miners they were by trade, country folk they were at heart.

Today the mines are closed – although the Swinhope Mine did not give up until as late as the 1960s. The big wheel at Sipton Mine has long been dismantled. The school, the church and two of the chapels have closed their doors for business, the latter now succumbing to the elements. Many of the miners' cottages, having stood empty and hollow for years, are now being refurbished and inhabited by "incomers".

The weather is probably the main topic of conversation, at least in winter. The dark months are fierce, harsh winds and icy blasts, snow drifts and blocked lanes. The arrival of the snow blower is a welcome sight, freeing the connection with the rest of the world, but as the dalesman watches the yellow hulk disappearing down the open tunnel of a road, frequently the track blows full again before dawn breaks.

Such a climate breeds hardy people. Tales of the '47 winter are still vividly recounted some 40 years on, photographs of the '63 storms are still passed around – the helicopter dropping food, folk standing on snow drifts topping the telegraph poles, vehicles snowbound, buried and marooned.

The idea to collect information about Sparty Lea was nurtured as I wandered around the village and the surrounding fells when I would come across ruined cottages, some now simply piles of stones, and wonder who had once called them home. The school, which we called home, harbours tales and reminiscences by the score. Ex-pupils and teachers alike have come through our front door and added to the treasury of memories of bygone days at "the school on the hill".

Then I met Mr Willie Parker, a retired farmer in his 80s and not only very able but very willing to paint a picture of Sparty Lea as it had been since the turn of the century. He put all the families back into those empty houses for me and made them come alive in our conversations.

Before long word had spread that I was interested in the past, and more and more local folk would come with tales of yesteryear until eventually the puzzle started to unscramble. Enlightening days were spent in the County Records Office with school log books, parish registers and census returns, and invariably I would travel home with another piece of the jigsaw slotted into place but with a new question revealed and awaiting solution by one Sparty Lea fireplace or another as the sun settled behind the upland fells.

Much of the material in this book arrived into my hands with the words: "I hear you're collecting old things." It was exactly in this way that I came across the original Cow Club book of 1858 whose President was Thomas Sopwith; the diaries of the indefatigable John Joseph Varty; and the memorable account of the horrendous winter of 1947 in one of the highest communities in England.

Having amassed so much information it seemed a pity to keep it to myself because what I had was a collection of snippets of history which had lain dormant in people's cupboards for decades and which other folk would take pleasure in sharing.

This is no more or less than a collection of information and, I would guess, a very incomplete collection at that. There are bound to be people who can lay their hands on lots more snippets lying in their cupboards or in their memories. All that I aspire to have done is to set my diverse collection under one cover.

If you are related to, or simply know, the Sparty Lea folk your interest will be immediately aroused. If you have never heard of Sparty Lea I hope you will be able to glean something of the lives of a dales leadmining community and feel the desire to come and see for yourself.

You will be assured of a warm welcome.

Jennifer W Norderhaug
Sparty Lea
January 1988

Johnny Pigg from Hillside walking along Sparty Lea Terrace with the Chapel and Miley's coal depot behind him.

Sparty Lea c.1900

St.Peter's Mine, Sparty Lea c.1900

St. Peter's Mine   1930

A group of washer lads standing in front of the jigging house at Sipton Mine c. 1914

Right:
Stone and wooden pit head buildings at Blackett Level Shaft top c. 1900

Sparty Lea with the old road over the ford before the bridge was built.

Sipton. From the left – Sipton Lead Mine, the mine manager's house, Sipton Terrace. The small building in the foreground was the gunpowder house.

Michael Elliott from Church Cottage, coalman and gravedigger for
St.Peter's Church. Locals came with horse and cart to collect their coal
from Miley's.

By the 1980s Miley's had become a garage for George Batey's car.
The tractor belongs to Tommy Borrowdale from High Hayrake.

Treasured Memories of the Allen Dales

The days are passing fast
And time is going by,
The changes they are mounting
In the valley neath the sky;
Yet as I walk the Allen's hillside
I still get me much joy,
In the memories of the times,
I walked there as a boy.

Then the tradesmen were working,
They came from near and far,
They came by foot and bicycle
And occasionally in a car;
Bill Dixon brought the groceries,
Jack Stephenson had his van;
Maggie Peart had the Post Office,
Willie Brown was butcherman.

Vernon Milburn took the orders
For Batches Week, at that,
Thirlwell Hutchinson delivered them
All with a horse and flat.
There was Humble from Wearhead
Got through in frost and fog,
Like Hill a constant traveller
Who once had a famous dog.

Through every storm that came,
Dickson Nichol delivered the mail;
And Johnny Charlton collected eggs
In a lorry from Allendale.
Kit Horncastle and Charlie Harrison
Travelled for animal needs,
Johnny Elliott with horse and cart
Delivered the animal feeds.

Rev Goodwin was the vicar
At St Peter's Church, Cornmill,
Thomas Bell was Headmaster;
At the school just up the hill,

Winnie Stoker was our teacher,
Her patience and beauty, a delight,
She came from Haydon Bridge
And hitch-hiked home each night.

Bob Batey kept the roads tidy,
Poor Bob, alas, we all say,
As in a balloon explosion
He died one fateful day;
Fred Sparke stoked the fires
In the Chapel at Sparty Lea,
While Alice Reed as caretaker
Kept as busy as a bee.

They worked the mine at Sipton
And the mine at Sparty Lea;
Ted Robinson was lorry driver
With rides he gave out free;
Ted Dodd was blacksmith,
Shod horses at the 'Heads each night,
While daytime at the mines
He worked with all his might.

Bob Walker was our bus driver,
Who was seldom ever late;
While Johnny Hepple was land agent
On his Lordship's estate.
The woodman was Tom Walker
His horse was strong and tall,
While Joe Wilkinson was mason,
Who answered our every call.

Matt Milburn was local builder,
He farmed at Huntwell,
As did Tom Graham and family,
Who built stone walls so well.
Vines and Fletcher were doctors,
Both said: "You go to bed",
Whether we had measles, coughs
Or just an aching head.

Hubert Dodd was wagon driver,
Took cattle to Hexham Mart;
Jim Noble collected milk,
At times with horse and cart.
Eddie Fairless was gamekeeper,
Assisted George Aikenhead,
They trod the moors and fells
Where the grouse and partridge bred.

Now I wander o'er the hillside,
And gaze across the dales,
As I watch the Allen flowing
On a course that never fails;
My thoughts do venture backwards,
And there give me much joy
In the people who were comrades
To a lonely little boy.

Lawrence Graham
1982

The Sparty Lea Flashlights football team c1950.
Back row; Raymond Archer, John Heslop, Eric Sanderson, Cyril Sparke
Middle row; John Sanderson, Colin Metcalf, Billy Pigg, Forster Milburn
Front row; Gordon Hutchinson, Albert Jackson, Willie Wright

The Use of Surnames in the Allen Valley

Surnames or family names have long been used in the area as middle or additional names and have usually indicated links of marriage.

Successive Lord Allendales were named Wentworth Blackett Beaumont recalling the Wentworth of Bretton Hall, Yorkshire – the family seat – and the Blacketts of Wallington and Newcastle whose heiress Diana married Col. Thomas Richard Beaumont.

On more ordinary levels, surnames were given also to denote links of marriage but were given, not as additional names, but as the sole Christian name.

One of the most common examples was the name Emerson. At the beginning of the century there were six men with the Christian name Emerson. This was not at all strange as Emerson was one of the most common surnames in Weardale. Indeed it was said that everyone in Weardale had the name Emerson, Peart or Featherstone. As the mines of Weardale and Allendale were jointly owned then, there was much intermixing in the partnerships of miners and so intimate friendships and intermarriage was common between the two dales. There was Emerson Ritson, Emerson Liddle, Emerson MacMillan or Em Sanderson and Em Humble.

Peart was another usual Weardale surname which was in use in the Allen Valley. Peart Heslop was a well known sporting character.

A Whitfield headmaster named Bell Dixon married into the Bell family. One of his wife's family (surname Bell) christened one of their sons Dixon. So there lived a Bell Dixon at Whitfield and a Dixon Bell at Catton. In later years there followed a Dixon Milburn and Dixon Nichol.

Sometimes two members of the same family would hold two different surnames as Christian names – for example the head of the Hull family at Huntwell was called Thompson Hull and his son was called Robson Hull. Also in the area there was Robson Rowell, Robson Pigg and Robson Reed.

There follows a list of local men with surnames for Christian names:

Nevin Reed	of	Coatinghill
Lowes Reed	of	Coalpits
Watson Milburn	of	Middlehope Green
Stephenson Stobbs	of	Elia

Errington Gibson	of	Ellershope
Tingate Varty	of	Coalpits
Shield Whitfield	of	Coalpits
Parker Liddle	of	Lot Head
Parker Wilson	of	Swinhope
Martin Wilson	of	Swinhope
Hewitson MacMillan	of	Guide Post

This use of surnames was not just a feature of the past. In later days the following names have existed: Thirlwell Hutchinson, Robinson Archer, Foster Parker, Chester Armstrong, Carr Bell, Henderson Fairless, Martin Jackson, Milton Forrest.

Although many Christian names were varied and distinctive, the majority were ordinary – John, Tom, Matt etc. In a small community of large families where two or three surnames predominated, there resulted in much confusion.

In 1886 Allendale Town had eight families of Dickensons, Sinderhope had six families of Charltons, Allenheads had eight families of Sparkes and seven of Milburns. There were 12 families of Reeds and 15 families of Philipsons. The result of this was that there were many people in the area, quite unrelated, with the same name. For instance, at one point there lived six different John Philipsons!

It became the practice then to distinguish one man from another by reference to his homestead. John Philipson of Bog House was known as Jack o' the Bogs, while another was Jack o' Tedham Green and another would be Johnny o' the Scotch Meadows.

Of the Reeds there was Jack o' the Hope Head (or Howp Head!), and Jack o' the Elpha Green.

There was Will o' the Rise Green, Tommy o' the Shield Bank, Willie o' the Old Dyke, Matt o' Sparty Lea, Nicol o' Byrehope, Jacob o' the Coatinghill and Isaac o' the Huntwell.

This was not restricted to men. Women with duplicating surnames were distinguished by abode too, for example, Jane Ann o' the Clay Hole and Jane Ann o' the Bank Top.

Mr Joseph Sparke, Sparty Lea

At 78 years of age Joseph Sparke is upright, bright and sprightly. He lives in a cottage out on the road beyond Allendale with his black cat and good neighbours for company.

This peaceful little pocket of Northumberland is a magic place where the haunting cry of the curlew echoes over the moors, and in dark quiet places the fox and the owl bid each other good-night.

Joseph first saw light of day at nearby Brackenhill, one of nine children born to Lily and Jack Sparke.

The lead mining industry was thriving then and Allendale and Allenheads were booming. Lord Allendale, who then owned the mines, also owned farms which he let to his workers.

Farmers usually kept a cow, a pig and some poultry, grew their own vegetables, made their own butter and in that way were self-sufficient and able to eat simply but well.

Jack worked in the mines and Lily, with the help of her growing family, worked the farm.

When he left the local St Peter's School, our Joseph went straight into the lead mines and then later worked on the farms. He wed a local girl and took up work on the roads doing kerbing and stone walling with some bridgework and quarrying.

A countryman then had to turn his hand to anything, was Joe's later verdict. He and his wife lived out a country life in the same place for 45 years, going to village fetes, village hops, whist drives, harvest festivals and the like.

Sadly Mrs Sparke died in 1980 and Joseph now relies on his surviving relatives for help and companionship. He reckons, as a widower, the saddest thing is the loss of friends as the years pass by.

The old schoolhouse still stands across the valley but the classrooms are silent now. Joseph can recall walking the winding country roads to school, passing the candle house where the miners' candles were made of yellow tallow with very strong wicks for use underground.

The lead mines were closed down when the price of lead fell disastrously low and the workforce was transferred to spar mines, spar being used in the steel/pottery industries. Spar was dressed at Allendale then taken away by rail from Catton for processing. Then gradually that came to an end.

Only a few chimneys stand now to remind passers-by that once a thriving community lived hereabouts. But the moors and hills are not lonely places. Farms nestle in nooks and crannies all about the landscape; fields are dotted with sheep and cattle and horses. Jolly chaps in Land Rovers give you a wave as they pass you on the road, their faces round and rosy. Smoke rises from cottage chimneys on coldish days, silence reigns supreme and at night the stars and the planets hang low in the sky.

Joseph Sparke can count himself a lucky countryman as he cycles down to Allenheads for a game of bowls and a chinwag with his friends.

Written by a lady holidaying in the next cottage to Mr Sparke
1986

Joe Sparke and Willie Parker at the Holms Linn Bridge, Sinderhope 1987

WARNING!
SNOWBLOWER
T.V. AERIAL ON RIGHT
EJECT SNOW TO LEFT

An early photo of Low Shield Close. Joe lived in the cottage on the right. The warning sign (inset) was erected by Joe in the field next to his cottage.

Joe Sparke in his garden with the bird house he built in 1988.

Mr Sparke

(In memoriam Annie Sparke, Joe's wife)

It was the worst winter in memory
his neighbour tells us, smoothing out
a cutting from the Hexham Courant –
a picture of already yellowing whiteness –
as if she thinks we don't believe her.

But we can see for ourselves: the grass
has hardly grown: spring flowers are late
coming through and in a dip beyond the far wood
there's a swathe of hard grey snow
with pine needles frozen in like splinters.

Up at Allenheads, she says, a man
who'd lived there all his life
and must have known the dangers
left his car and was buried in a drift
they thought he'd have to have his hand off.

She'd been worried Mrs Sparke
would wander out again and be lost
that's why she'd called the doctor.
her husband dug a tunnel to the phone box –
it was like standing in an igloo.

The snow was piled so high
they had to stand on chairs to watch
for the ambulance from the window.
And after that they were cut off for weeks.
He never saw her again.

Mr Sparke's garden is as trim as ever.
The narrow borders by the path
are lined with scarlet tulips;
the soil is freshly dug and raked
ready for potatoes and the first seeds.

Dressed in his dark blue Sunday suit
he called to us – not as we'd expected
to sit with him in gloomy sympathy
but to admire (what must have cost him most
of the insurance) a new cassette recorder.

At the centre of the old oak sideboard,
flanked by two china shepherdesses,
it seems oddly out of place.
Like a child showing off a new toy
he won't let us go until we've heard it.

We try to think of an excuse to go.
But suddenly like ice melting in a thaw
the sound begins to flow –
an accordion band squeezing out
'What a friend we have in Jesus'.

And Mr Sparke is crying; rubbing
at his eyes with work-swollen hand.
'What I always say is' he shouts
above the noise: 'It's my belief
that time's a great healer'.

Poem by Vicki Feaver from CLOSE RELATIVES, published by Secker 1981

Vicki was one of Joe's closest neighbours, living at Bank Top, Sparty Lea.

Thomas Archer, Joiner
Extracts from his Ledger 1899-1908

Thomas Archer was a joiner from Sinderhope and among the apprentices he trained were two young chaps from Sparty Lea, Jack Reed of Hope Head and Henry Robson of Old Dyke. After their five-year apprenticeship Jack and Henry later took over the business as Reed and Robson on 19th October 1908. Thomas was to die before the Great War started.

Henry's son Herbert kindly loaned the account book.

1899	Sparty Lea Chapel			
	Wood for top seats 1 - 16ft 6in x 1in		1s	4d
	Top rail for seat 1 - 3ft 1 - 6in x 1in			4d
	Window bottom wood 7ft x 1in			7d
	Repairing window & capping 22ft			8d
	Wood for hat rails 40ft 1.5 x 1 3/4in		1s	8d
	Front D frames 1 splice 3in x 3in			4d
	1 crate of oak varnish		1s	4d
	Outside gate both huns spliced			
	2 splices 1ft long		2s	0d
	1 new bottom rail 2.1in long 3in x 2in			
	1 new round upright			
	New sash cord for 2 windows			6d
	1 new sash fastener			7d
	Varnishing cupboard		1s	0d
	Repairing window, new sill, rep jambs		5s	6d
	Labour for repairing inside ceiling		5s	6d
	Wood for ceiling 22ft of 6 in x 1in		2s	9d
		£1	4s	1d
	Contract for varnishing & painting inside of Chapel 2 crates	3	15s	1d
Jan 26	Settled	£4	19s	2d
Jan 5	Mr Nicholas Lee, Breckon Holme			
	4 wheels for hay rack @ 1s 4d each		5s	4d
	2 axles @ 2s 6d each		4s	10d
	140 iron rods at 1d each		11s	8d
Mar 4	4 deals 12ft 6in x 11in x 1/2in RW 50 @ 3d p ft		12s	6d
	Settled			

1908				
Nov 24	Hexham Rural District Council			
	Painting Swinhope Bridge	£1	0s	0d
	Settled			
1909				
Nov 11	New foot bridge all pitch pine 20ft long	£3	13s	3d
	Settled			
July	Repairs to Sparty lea bridge			
	material & labour		5s	3d

1908				
Dec 5	Nicholas Lee, Coal Pitts			
	1 new window painted & hung complete	£1	0s	0d
	Painting entrance to house 2 colours		6s	0d
	Varnishing ceiling making 1 large		1s	6d
	drawer for cupboard & supplying			
	wood for front		4s	2d
	Fixing 2 night latches & putting on knobs		1s	3d
	Painting 4 windows 1 coat @ 9d each gate		3s	6d
1910				
Mar 7	Settled	£1	16s	5d

1908				
Dec 4	Nevin Reed, Coating Hill			
	2 panes of glass		1s	4d
	Settled			

1909				
Jan	John H Robson, Ellershope			
	1 new press			
	2 tables kitchen & round	£10	14s	6d
	1 corner bed 4 chairs			
	Settled			

1910				
April 25	1 wash stand & dressing table	£6	0s	0d
	Settled			
	7 pictures framed	£1	2s	0d
Aug 5	Settled			

1909				
July 10	J W Robson, Shield Bank			
	1 pair of new wheels	£3	18s	0d
	1 new iron gate	£1	7s	0d
	Settled	£5	5s	0d

1909				
May 28	William Renwick, Hunt Well			
	1 butter box		10s	9d
	Settled			

	J Bell, Guide Post			
	1 swingle tree		2s	0d
	Settled			
	1 pitch pine coffin, electro brass mounts	£3	5s	0d
Aug 1910	Settled			

1910				
Oct	Swinhope Chapel Trustees			
	Painting all windows spouting &			
	graining 2 doors & painting door			
	inside as tender	£2	3s	0d
Dec 22	Settled			

1909				
Dec 21	Parker Liddle, Sipton			
	1 new corner bed		13s	0d
	Settled			

	Hearse Committee			
	Repairs to hearse door bottom rail		6s	0d
	1 set harness hook 7ft long		2s	6d
	repairs to stand		1s	3d
	1 tassel repaired		1s	6d
	repairs to lift		1s	6d
	Settled		12s	9d

Nov 11	County Council, St Peter's School			
	2 panes of glass put in		4s	6d
	1 glass panel in door		2s	6d
1910	Settled			
1910 July	St Peter's School Colourwashing all external & internal painting & varnishing	£13	1s	5d
Oct 1	Paid			
Aug	St Peter's School Repairs to ceiling & putting 4 new slates in roof		5s	0d
Oct 31	Paid			

1910	Matthew H Reed, Sipton			
	1 new cart coup	£2	5s	0d
	Settled			
1910 July 26	2lbs green paint		1s	2d
Sept 12	Paid			

1909 June 19	Messrs Nobles, Corn Mill 1 new coup painting wheels & shafts ironwork	£2	10s	6d
1910	Settled			
Dec 22	1 new sheep rack	£2	3s	6d
Mar 17	Trap repaired new shafts etc & repainted & varnished	£3	19s	2d
May 10	Settled	£6	2s	8d
May 27	1 cart jack repaired		1s	0d
July 1	1 new rake		1s	6d
	1 new steel 1 new head 2 bows others fastened		2s	9d
Aug	Bogie repaired		1s	0d

Aug 27	Cart repaired new block		8s	0d
	new limmer bar in oak		3s	6d
		£1	0s	9d

1909				
July 17	John Philipson, Coatin Hill			
	Putting beam in roof & 4lb of nails		3s	6d
	Settled			
1910				
Feb 21	1 new cart wheel	£1	0s	0d
	Settled			
July 6	1 hay sled repaired new sides		8s	3d

June 1	J R Stephenson, Stripe House, Swinhope			
	1 closet put in		13s	0d
	14ft shelving put in pantry		6s	8d
	1 new lock put on		2s	9d
	Taking out corner bed		2s	0d
	5 blind rollers upstairs		5s	0d
	& alterations at stair head		4s	9d
	1 loose pane hinged		2s	6d
	new pin sail		1s	3d
	door to bedroom put on complete		9s	0d
	Platform for piano		4s	0d
	Spars 2in x 2in for		7s	6d
	Middlehope		6s	3d
	casement fastener		1s	6d
		£2	18s	4d
Nov	Settled			

1909				
Nov 11	Messrs Charltons, Burn Foot			
	1 pitch pine coffin in electro			
	brass mounts	£3	18s	6d
	Disinfecting and papering room	£1	6s	3d
		£5	4s	9d
	Dis		1s	3d
	Settled	£5	3s	6d

John Joseph Philipson Varty at the Burnfoot Show, Allenheads.

An early photograph of the Burnfoot Show showing the Allenheads Silver Band
3rd from left (in bowler) Joe Bill Philipson,
& far right (light cap) Tom Graham, Huntwell

John Joseph Philipson Varty

John Joseph Varty was born in 1865 at Green Pitts, Sparty Lea.

He grew up in the Sparty Lea area and attended St Peter's Board School for ONE HALF DAY in his life. Local legend states that having been caned on his first morning, unfairly he thought, he took the decision to "terminate his formal education".

I stress this point because as you read the following extracts from his diaries from 1902 and 1905 it seems incredible to believe that this man had no official schooling.

His writing is immaculate, the spelling good with only one or two errors, his attention to detail is exemplary and his involvement in the community in an organising capacity denotes an active and thinking mind.

He displays the farmer's keen meteorological interest to the extent of a daily weather report which, for a time, even includes a daily barometer reading.

His life was obviously varied and rarely idle as a hill farmer with sheep and cattle and all the work which that way of life entailed.

In 1893 he formed a social club in his own home at Green Pitts, Sparty Lea, for the pleasure of the men and youngsters in the area. There they gathered every weekend to play dominoes, darts, quoits or shooting. Records are meticulously kept of scores and prize winners.

Added to this hobby John Joseph was Secretary and Treasurer of the local Burnfoot Show for many years and the programme of the 1924 event shows again his attention and care for local detail.

He was a frequent visitor to Willie Parker's farm at Scotch Meadows (the same Mr Parker I speak of in the 1947 winter chapter) and Willie remembers him as "a good crack" with lots of imaginative stories to tell.

His presence was usually seen at all the local picnics, social events and agricultural shows and, on occasion, he even walked over to the Grasmere Sports in Cumbria.

He married Mary Elizabeth McMillan from Sparty Lea and they had five children – Annie, Maria, Matthew, Herbert and Joe.

Today his grandsons, Derek and Edward, remember him as an active, elegant man. His house is still occupied, having been renovated, although his club and the Burnfoot Show have long since disappeared.

John Joseph Varty died on 24th May 1953 at the age of 88 years. His wife, aged 78, had died seven years previously.

There follow extracts from two of John Joseph Varty's diaries from 1902 and 1905 kindly loaned by his grandson Derek Varty. Derek was brought up at Lot Head in Sparty Lea but now lives in Hexham near to his elderly father, Herbert.

John Joseph makes reference twice to a Doctor's Club. This was the early National Health whereby people paid an annual sum to the local doctor to take care of call outs, medicine, etc. In Sparty Lea there were two clubs available to join – one in Weardale and one in Allendale. The fact that John Joseph's first son, Matthew, was born at Wearhead would suggest that the Vartys paid into the Weardale doctor's club.

There was also a Cow Club into which farmers paid a certain sum and if they lost a beast they could claim compensation from the club. The first club in the area was set up at Allenheads in 1858 under the patronage of Wentworth Blackett Beaumont MP and the chairmanship of Thomas Sopwith.

Although John Joseph Varty makes no mention of paying into it, it would be feasible to assume that he, like most other farmers, would be a member.

Extracts from John Joseph Varty's Diary 1902

Friday 3 Jan	*Showery day. Light roan cow calved – light roan bull calf. At the club: shooting championship won by T. Sanderson.*
Sat 4 Jan	*Sold little cow to Mr W Milburn. Shooting at night.*
Sat 11 Jan	*Hard frost. Thomas Armstrong found dead in bed at Huds Riding.*
Sat 8 Feb	*Frost and snow. At the shooting at night won the special prize. M Nixon won the 20 shots record with a score of 96. He also won the 10 shots standing record. J Reed won the medal for lads 10 shots record with a score of 48. S Philipson won the Hook It Board. This brought the shooting season to a very successful close. M Nixon won the club gun.*
Sat 15 Feb	*H Sanderson to P Ann Peart (married).*
Wed 19 Feb	*Still hard frost and snow.*
Wed 26 Feb	*Hard frost. 8 carts of manure.*
Sat 1 March	*Fine frosty morning. Ping Pong and football match Rookhope 1 Allenheads 0.*
Thurs 6 March	*Fresh dull day. Manure carting 4 cartfulls. Total 33.*
Sat 8 March	*Rain. At Scotsmeadows sale (Elliotts) a very dear sale. Cows:*

Cows:

April calver 8 years old	*£14.7.6*
Heifer July calver	*£14.17.6*
Calver heifer 8 weeks old	*£3.17.0*
Steer	*£3*
Stirk	*£7.17.6*
Horse	*£19.10.0*

Sat 15 March	*Cold day with showers of hail. At Allendale Town at football match between Allendale Town team and the*

Allenheads team – Allendale Town won by 4 goals to nil.

Wed 19 March

Dull cold raw morning. Manure carting 4 cartfulls. Total 37 for the Spring.

Fri 21 March

Windy morning. Snow falling and the sun shining. Joe Graham. At Ping Pong at night. Walking stick arrived.

Sat 22 March

Hot sun but hard frost. Snow all gone at Green Pitts in the afternoon. Dr Murray presented with a walking stick by the AHCC

Mon 24 March

Cold raw day snow fell heavy during the afternoon. At T Dodds Allenheads in the afternoon getting the pony shod.

Sat 29 March

Sale of guns in stock. No 3 Jeffrey air gun 20/0d. Newspapers Weekly Leader, Hexham Courant and the Sunday Chronicle. At the football match at Allenheads between Allenheads and the down by section of the Allenheads club the same resulted in a draw after a very evenly played game. The day was severe cold with heavy showers of snow and rain at intervals.

Sat 5 April

Nice frost morning at 7. At a football match at Allenheads between Allenheads and Allendale Town resulted in a draw 2 goals each. Heavy showers of snow during the progress of the game. John Philipson to Miss Jane Nixon.

Mon 7 April

Fine cold morning at 9a.m. Manure spreading concluded. Paid J Craig 3/8d for Doctor's Club.

Thurs 10 April

Beautiful morning at 11a.m. Dyking.

Mon 14 April

Fine spring morning. Planting potatoes 2 rows of roses and 4 of whites.

Sat 19 April

Fine spring morning. Fine day at Swinhope Bazaar opened at 6p.m. by Mrs Ritson. Partridge nest BM.

Sat 26 April	*Dry cold day. Cricket match at Allenheads. Allenheads 27 Westgate 17.*
Wed 30 April	*Cold windy day. 12 gooseberry bushes cut.*
Thur 1 May	*Cold dull morning. Idle day.* *R Glendinning to Isa Roddam.*
Sat 3 May	*Soft morning. At Jim Hutchinson's sale cows £16.10.0 to £19, calved heifers 17 to 18, top prize heifer calves £1.12.6 to £3. Bought wood for 4/3.* *J Reed Elpha to Miss Martha Parker.*
Mon 5 May	*Cold day. At T Dodds. Paid J Parker 15/0 for cow serving.*
Sat 10 May	*J Wall to E Jane Short.*
Wed 14 May	*Cold day. Planting potatoes.*
Mon 19 May	*Cold showery day. At Hexham Sports a very enjoyable day.*
Sat 24 May	*Splendid spring day. Allenheads CC beat Westgate.*
Mon 26 May	*Showery day. Sowing turnips.*
Fri 30 May	*Cold east wind. Barrow making. At the Burnfoot Show. Meeting at St Peter's Board School.*
Mon 2 June	*Soft morning. At Allenheads at the cinomatagraph entertainment.*
Thur 5 June	*Cold raw. House cleaning. Peace proclaimed.*
Sat 7 June	*Cold heavy rain. Sparty Lea Pic nic.* *J Pigg to Miss Dargue.*
Tue 10 June	*Cold Nor Easter. Peat cutting.*
Sat 22 June	*Beautiful morning. Odd jobs. At a cricket match at AH ground between Whitfield and Allenheads. Allenheads 48 Whitfield 47. Beautiful day.*

Thurs 26 June	*Beautiful morning. Coronation day. At the Sports held on the cricket field. J Sanderson's 11 won the cricket match. J Sanderson first for wrestling, Joe Parker 2nd and J Johnson 3rd. W Robson won the Footrace, J Sanderson 2nd and H Kell 3rd. Splendid day although.*
Mon 30 June	*Beautiful morning. Bar 7½ 70. Peat setting and turnip thinning.*
Sat 5 July	*Beautiful morning. Extra hot. Carting lime and sand etc. Allenheads CC beat Lanehead.*
Mon 7 July	*Dull windy day. At Catton for 10½cwt of Mick coal for 8/0d.*
Tues 8 July	*Rain with a west wind. Bar 7½. At Allenheads Paid J Craig ¾ for Doctor's club.*
Wed 9 July	*Rain. At Catton Coals got 7cwt of Clara Vale coal for 8/3. Bar 3½ 68 - 8.20. - 2.30.*
Thurs 10 July	*Cold damp morning. B3. At Catton for 10cwt of Walbottle coal for 7/6. Record day for rain 1/30 7/30*
Fri 11 July	*Fine morning. At the Royal Show at Carlisle. Spent a very interesting day.*
Wed 16 July	*Beautiful morning at 5a.m. Got one cart of peats in the forenoon and cut a set of grass in the low pasture in the afternoon.*
Sat 2 Aug	*Rain. B6 60f. Morpeth Sports held today.*
Mon 4 Aug	*Warm at 6. Rain at 3p.m. Bar 5. Hexham Show held today.*
Thurs 7 Aug	*Rain. Cutting rushes. At White Hill with the young roan cow.*

Sat 9 Aug	*Cold fine day up to 4p.m. when rain fell. Half day at the hay. Coronation day.*
Sat 23 Aug	*Allendale Town Show day. Cut north corner high half. Half day carted four pikes.*
Wed 3 Sept	*At St John's Chapel twice on account of Dr Wolf. Dark misty morning followed by a blizzard of a day. A male child born at 9.30a.m. B1½. Matthew.*
Sat 6 Sept	*Bents Show Day. A fine dull day. Carting hay 7 pikes.*
Sat 13 Sept	*Fine day. Stanhope Show.*
Fri 19 Sept	*Beautiful morning. At Burnfoot Show won first prize in the Open and also the 25 acre class for Best Heifer above one year old and under two with a red heifer third in the two year old heifer class and 3rd in the teapot class. Altogether a very enjoyable day.*
Sat 20 Sept	*Fine dull day at Allenheads District Sports. The Sports were a success.*
Wed 24 Sept	*Cutting and rakeing rushes. Fine day althrough.*
Mon 29 Sept	*Dull morning. At Catton got 10¾cwt of Clara Vale coal 9/6d. Also a hamper of plums 3/9d apples total 5/0d.*
	New rules for Shooting Club Arranged for 1902 – 3 John J Varty Secretary and Treasurer
Sat 18 Oct	*Fine day at Dovespool. Shooting at night. Alston Fair day.*
Wed 22 Oct	*Manure carting to the pastures 5 cartfulls. Cold day. E Charlton to H E Ridley.*
Tues 28 Oct	*Fine morning potatoe lifting.*
Sat 8 Nov	*Heavy rain. At Bellah Roddam's sale Mill Cottages.*

Wed 12 Nov	*Fine day. Turnip lifting.*
Wed 19 Nov	*Cold day extra frost. Gun arrived from Gamage by rail cost £1.15s.0d. The gun is a Militia Air Rifle and very accurate at a fair distance. Paid 6d for stamps.*
Fri 21 Nov	*Hard frost but fine and dry. At the club at night – results George Vickers won the cows at Quoits with a score of 58. H Shield won candlesticks at 48. James Pearson won a dominoe competition for a silk tie. Matt Nixon 2nd. Local ex – 6d. A splendid night's sport over 20 persons present. Shooting, dominoe playing and Quoits comprizeing the programme.*
Sun 7 Dec	*Cold day with snow. At DP PMC A. Anderson preacher. (Dirt Pot Primitive Methodist Chapel)*
Thur 11 Dec	*Fair fresh wind. Bought a dog named Hall from Robt Curry Stripe House for 30/0d.*
Fri 12 Dec	*Fine frosty day. At the club at night. Large attendance. M Nixon won a picture of Holms Lynn.*
Thur 25 Dec	*Nice forenoon. At the annual shooting in the afternoon won first prize a set of Carriers score 47 in ten shots. Also won Jack in Box shooting. At a Magic Lantern and supper at the club.*
Wed 31 Dec	*Snow on the ground to a depth of about 2 inches. Cold NorEaster.*
REMARKS	*It may be noted as one of the coldest dampest days on record the local shows the Pic nics lucky for fine days all of which were a decided success the two Coronation days extra fine.*

Extracts from John Joseph Varty's Dairy 1905

Sunday 8 Jan	Nice dull day. Read "A Master Rogue" by Edgar Pickering, "The Youngest Miss Brown" by Florence Warden, "The Fatal Kiss" by Kit Dealtry.
Saturday 14 Jan	Club shooting adjourned on account of the Brass Band Social at Allenheads.
1 Feb	Bought silk square and stockings.
Saturday 29 April	Showery day. Newcastle won the League Championship.
Saturday 13 May	Beautiful day. Took two stints for one year at 5sh each belonging to M W Milburn.
Saturday 3 June	Beautiful day. Idle Day. Thomas Pigg to Maggie Philipson.
Wednesday 7 June	Cold dry day. Sent for the silver cup for the pic nic.
Saturday 17 June	Beautiful day at Rookhope Pic Nic small attendance. Cricket competition: Lanehead 1 Allenheads 2.
Wednesday 21 June	Showery day. Sold a bedstead and bought a barrel.
Thursday 22 June	The most beautiful day of the year. Paid Miss Lizzie Renwick for bacon £7-7-0.
Tuesday 11 July	Beautiful day. At the Kiln got 4 load of lime 4-0d. Soled a pair of boots.
Wednesday 19 July	Beautiful day. At Catton for an American rake – left 5a.m. home at 11 a.m. Sparty Lea at 10a.m. Won the East, the West and the Front fields.
Wednesday 9 August	At Hexham got a trap from J Cowan. Showery.
Thursday 31 August	Beautiful morning. Peace declared between Russia and Japan at 4p.m. yesterday.

Tuesday 5 Sept	*Fine day with a shower at 12. Left for Hexham at 7.15a.m. arrived in Hexham at 10.30. Left Hexham at 6p.m. arrived home at 9.20.*
Tuesday 19 Sept	*Beautiful day. At Hexham Auction Mart Harry's cow made £18.15.0. Splendid day.*
Saturday 30 Sept	*Fine but cold. At Mrs Watson's sale at Sidehead, Weardale. Good sale cows up to £16, heifer due October 28 £9, calf up to £5, mare £8, foal £5.*
Saturday 21 October	*Cold day with snow. At a sale at Keenley South Leazes bought a ton of hay for £4.10.0, a barn of hay for £6.15.0 at Sparks Middle Hay Leazes.*
Tuesday 31 October	*Fine day. At Hall Keenley got 174 stone of hay left at 7 home at 5. Splendid hay cost.*
Thursday 9 Nov	*Fine morning at Keenley for two loads of hay. Left home at 6a.m. home at 3p.m.*
Friday 10 Nov	*Fine day. Pig butchered by Thompson Lee weight 19½stones.*
Saturday 11 Nov	*Wet day. Pig work.*
Friday 24 Nov	*Nice fresh day. Received the air gun from Johnson Hexham cost 5/0d.*
Wednesday 13 Dec	*Nice soft day. Bought a tie 1/0d silk tie 1/6d.*
Tuesday 19 Dec	*Paid George Philipson 5/0d for the red cow bulling.*

Hexham Mart milk cows:
1	*F Smith Simonburn*	*£24.0.0*
2	*Mrs Ord Haining Rigg*	*£22.2.6*
3	*W Teasdale Hawkuplea*	*£21.10.0*
	N Ridley and T Dodd Judges	

Monday 25 Dec	*Xmas Day. No shooting at the club – first day missed since the formation of the club in 1893.*

Wednesday 27 Dec   *Paid 8/0d for sundries (bleezor 4/6, clamps etc 3/6)*

REMARKS   *It may be said to have been a very remarkable year, the early part of the summer was extra hot and very little rain. The latter part of summer was wet and cold the pic nics was favoured with beautiful days. Visits to Hexham, Rookhope and Allenheads and Burnfoot Pic nics, Woodhead and Haydon Bridge were well enjoyed. Visits to Hexham Show, Allendale Town Bents St Johns and Stanhope miserable days with no enjoyment. Burnfoot Show a record success. Mr H Pigg took Cherry down to the show and got second prize. Aston Villa won the English Cup Newcastle United second won by 2 goals to nil – attendance 101,000.*

The Cornmill with the wheel visible. St. Peter's Vicarage can be seen in the
background c1900.

The Cornmill Show c1900.

The Cornmill Show

As early as 1882 there are entries in St Peter's School log book that the school was closed due to the children being given holiday to attend the Cattle Show and Sheep Fair at the Corn Mill. The head teacher refers to it as "the greatest day of the year". In 1938 the Hexham Courant reports at length on one "of the oldest agricultural fixtures in the North" – the Corn Mill Show. In the article which follows I have included, from a long list of prize winners, the successful entrants from the Sparty Lea area.

In the 1880s Mr W B Beaumont sanctioned that a fair be held at the Corn Mill twice a year on a Friday in Spring and Autumn. A charge was to be made to the tenant of the showground:

> one penny per head of cattle
> one penny for a sheep
> six pennies for a cart load of pigs
> various charges for roundabouts and stalls

There was also an inn at the Corn Mill until the turn of the 19th century which no doubt helped the ambiance of the fair day enormously. Photographs do exist of the doorway to the Mill with an inn sign hanging above it and a gathering of folk at the Show which was held just to the right of the house and buildings at the foot of Chapel Row, the footpath from the Mill to the School bank.

Hexham Courant Report for the Cornmill Show of 1938

Extracts:

SWALEDALE'S GAIN IN POPULARITY
RECORD ENTRY AT NORTH'S OLDEST SHOW

Reputed to be the oldest agricultural fixture in the North, the 143rd exhibition of the Allenheads Agricultural Society held at Corn Mill Allenheads on Saturday had a record entry in a day of mixed weather.

Notable features of the show were the Swaledale sheep classes and the Industrial section. Classes which were introduced into the show in 1924 have met with success since.
ALLENHEADS SUCCESS

The show was held in a field kindly placed at the disposal of the Society by Messrs Nichol and Mr J P Noble.

Rain fell heavily in the morning but after mid day conditions greatly improved and while there were fitful intervals of sunshine the remainder of the day was pleasant. In view of the weather conditions the attendance was satisfactory.
At Saturday's show competition among blackfaces was chiefly confined to Mr M H Reed and Mr J Shield, both local exhibitors of note who divided the prizes between them. The special for the group prize was taken by Mr J Shield. Swaledales on the other hand had a big average. A claim worthy of mention is an entry of 12 gimmer lambs in the district section which were all paraded before the judges. Mr J V Peart's aged ram with many wins to its credit stood first in its class. The ewes were outstanding but altogether the Swaledales formed a remarkably good show.
Shorthorns were lighter than usual and in the Young Farmers class Miss L M Hull's exhibit which has gained a showyard record this season stood first.
Horses both for general purposes and dales ponies were a small show.

INDUSTRIAL RECORDS

In dairy produce the classes for eggs made a good display. The industrial section had an increased entry of 125 constituting a record. The special for the best exhibit in the section was given to a chipped wool hearthrug shown by Mrs J C Hutchinson of Pineville Allendale. Competing in the industrial department were many well known successful exhibitors at other local shows. Among the vegetable classes was an excellent show of produce.
E Wilkinson of Catton was the most successful exhibitor in the open classes, gaining 13 first prizes and 4 seconds.

The judges were: Cattle, Mr Collinson; blackfaced sheep, Mr E Maddison; Swaledale sheep and dogs, Mr W W Peacock, Westgate; Bread, eggs and jams, Mrs G Dodd, Allendale, Miss K Shortridge, Allendale; Industrial section, Mrs Chambers, Allendale, Mrs Hepple, Allenheads, Mrs Pape, Nenthead, Miss Routledge, Nenthead; Vegetables and flowers, Mr MacGowan, Consett. The secretarial duties were efficiently discharged by Mr A Nixon, who officiated in that capacity for the first time.

Some local winners:

BLACKFACED SHEEP:
Aged tup: 1 M H Reed, Sipton. 3 J Parker, Burnfoot.
Shearling tup: 1 M H Reed.
Tup lamb: 1 M H Reed. 2 John Shield. 3 M H Reed.
Ewe that has reared a lamb this season: 1 M H Reed. 2 John Shield.
Shearling gimmer: 1 & 2 John Shield. 3 M H Reed.
SWALEDALE SHEEP (District):
Aged tup: 1 M M Armstrong. 2 F Hutchinson.
Shearling tup: 1 R Johnson. 2 M M Armstrong.
Shearling gimmers: 1 R Johnson. 2 Mrs Short & Son.
Gimmer lamb: 1 F Hutchinson. 2 Mrs Short & Son.
SHORTHORN CATTLE:
Cow in milk: 1 Messrs John Henderson & Son. 2 W Glendinning, Pry Hill.
Heifer to retain its calf teeth: 2 T Graham, Hunt Well.
Heifer calf under one year: 1 Miss L M Hull, Swinhope Shield.
YOUNG FARMER'S CLASS (open to clubs in Northumberland & Durham):
Calf: 1 Miss L M Hull.
HORSES:
General purpose horse: 2 M Milburn, Huntwell. 3 J W Robson.
DOGS (open):
Rough coated collie dog or bitch: 2 T J Robson, Low Swinhope Shield
Smooth coated collie dog or bitch: 1 Elsom Robson. 2 M Milburn.
DAIRY PRODUCE (open):
Six white hen eggs: 2 J C Sanderson, Hill Side.
BAKING (open):
Loaf of white bread: 1 Mrs D Nichol, Water house.
Plain tea cake: 2 Mrs Philipson, Tedham Green.
Spice girdle cake: 1 Mrs A Nixon.
Dish of tea pastries: 1 & 2 Mrs J Parker.
HONEY & JAM (open):
Bottle of rhubarb wine: 1 Mrs T J Robson.
CHILDREN'S SECTION:
Bunch of wild flowers: 1 Maureen Hull. 2 Derek Nichol.
Needlework: 1 Isobel Dixon. 2 Dorothy Bell.
Needlework for girls under 10: 1 A Littlefair. 2 June Reed.
Knitted article for girls under 10: 1 Joyce Renwick. 2 S Ridley.
Handwork boys over 10: 1 A Bright. 2 E Renwick.
Handwork boys under 10: 1 Laurie Graham.
Pencil drawing beech spray: 1 G R Philipson. 2 R Graham.

Dales of Allen

Oh, Dales of Allen, hear us sing your praise!
You were our home, our world, in childhood's days!
In you, spread out before our infant gaze,
We found a Fairyland of Elfin ways.
In youth we climbed your hills with tireless feet,
O'er fell and moorland, heather, bog and peat;
And swam the pool where both bright Allens meet
When hearts were young, and limbs were lithe and fleet.

Could there, in all the world, be Dales more dear
To those who long the curlew's call to hear,
To breathe the upland breezes, fresh and clear,
While tumbling burns make music to the ear?
Oh, lovely Dales, how we for you did yearn,
When far from you we fared, our bread to earn
But in our hearts we said, "We will return,
And make, in those fair Dales, our last sojourn.

E.S. Gaskin

This poem was written by the late Elizabeth Shield Gaskin of Allendale

Winter's Truth

The golden hues of Autumn
The purple heather's bloom
Belie the wrath which plunges
The dale into winter's gloom.

Morning mists, September softness,
A gentle whisper o'er the fell
Change to December madness
With a fury straight from Hell.

Hay supplies which dwindle
With the shortening of the days;
Larders filled with groceries
In the winter stock-up craze.

Icy blasts, drifts and blizzards
As the year begins anew.
Ewes buried, morning searches,
Frozen fingers, nerves askew.

Helicopters to the rescue -
Drifts topping the telegraph pole.
The drone of plough and blower
An open road their only goal.

There's another side to the uplands
That the tourist doesn't see.
An uncharitable stillness,
A harsh reality.

A winter picture postcard
A dream of shimmering white
Has a truth that only Dales folk
Have the stamina to fight.

Even the 63 and 47
Dalers managed to survive
It's the strong community spirit
Which keeps the hills alive.

Alive to fight the tantrums
Which the elements can fling,
Until, all anger past and spent,
A morning breaks to the sound of Spring.

Jennifer Norderhaug 1987

The Last Journey of Thomas Parker Liddell
(1879 – 1916)

Parker Liddell was a local lad brought up at Ellershope in Sparty Lea.

He took to the lead mines for employment together with his friends and became employed in the Nenthead mines.

As a young man he married a local girl, Mary Robson from the Old Dyke. They lived for a short while on Sipton Terrace before settling at Lot Head where they had a smallholding, as was the custom among the miners, to supplement their income.

Mary and Parker had six children, some of them still surviving at the time of writing.

It could not have been easy for the parents, their home isolated high up on the fells with water to be drawn from a well and only a rough track leading from the steep, narrow bank which quickly fills up with snow in winter.

It was in such dreadful weather conditions in March 1916 that Parker Liddell set off for work at Nenthead. It was to be the last time he would make the outward journey from his little cottage where his wife and brood were safely sheltered against the elements rampaging around them.

The accident in the mine that March day was long to be remembered. The fall of stone injured Parker and his fellow miners, thinking he would receive better medical attention at Nenthead than Carrshield, carried him through four miles of underground mine workings until they could surface at the Rampgill Shaft. Four days later Parker died from pneumonia.

As Mary waited, grieving with her family at Sparty Lea, the men of two valleys swung into action to bring Parker's body back home to the churchyard of St Peter's.

Around 40 Nenthead men pulled the coffin on a hand-drawn sledge to Coalcleugh where they were met by a similar number of Sparty Lea men. The sad party drew their friend and neighbour through the driving blizzard over some of England's highest and bleakest moors to the tiny graveyard by the river.

But the ordeal was not over. When the men turned to leave the churchyard, snow already filling the open grave, they realized that one of their men, Mr Price, was nowhere to be seen. Somehow he had become separated from the party on the treacherous fell top. So the men made their way back once more into the fury of the storm. It was the next day when they finally sighted the lone man wandering the moors, totally lost, in Weardale.

Mary Liddell reared her brood of six in the lonely cottage high on the moors with help from her nephews down in Sparty Lea. One of those nephews, Herbert Robson, remembers his aunt as a cheerful, resourceful woman who would often walk over the fields down to the village for company. She lived to a good old age despite the cruel blow which took her young husband from her in such tragic circumstances.

The entry in St Peter's churchyard book reads simply:

Thomas Parker Liddell, Lot Head. Buried 12 March 1916 aged 37 years.
No hearse charge.

What a wealth of human endeavour lies behind those words.

Lot Head – This is where Parker and his wife Mary started their family.
The house stands high above Sparty Lea at about 1,200ft.

First left – Robinson Archer, Second from right – Willie Parker.

Scotchmeadows – The home of Willie Parker and his family in 1947.

The Winter of 1947

There follow some extracts from the diary of a hill farmer trying to survive the worst winter in living memory on one of the more remote farmsteads above Sparty Lea.

Willie Parker was born at Sinderhope in 1903. Son of a farmer, he left the local Sinderhope school at the age of 13 and spent some years lead mining in Sipton and St Peter's mines before eventually getting his own tenancy at Scotchmeadows.

Scotchmeadows lies in the shadow of Killhope Law towering to a height of 2,000 feet. The farm supported sheep and dairy cattle with stints on the outlying fells.

Willie and his wife Hilda had two sons, Ronnie and Kenneth, and a daughter Lorna.

In the 1950s Willie moved his family to farm at Brampton where they stayed for 17 years. His sons still farm the family acres but Willie came back to Sparty Lea to retire in a cottage on Sparty Lea Terrace.

For some years he was a Parish Councillor, involved in all the local work and he is now Chairman of the Churchyard Fund - a group of local men who tend and tidy the churchyard in their spare time. He is the proud owner of a congratulatory telegramme from Her Majesty the Queen for the occasion of his diamond wedding anniversary; he has a marvellous collection of old local photographs and a memory and love for retelling tales from times past that shows his heartfelt fondness for the Dale.

Without Willie this book would not have been considered or possible. Many cosy evenings spent "blathering" over his warming hearth have laid the foundations for this collection of memories from Sparty Lea. His tape recordings of days gone by are part of my treasured possessions.

Extracts from Mr Willie Parker's Diary 1947

Scotchmeadows, Sparty Lea

Thursday 9 Jan	*Ronnie went off to Nova Scotia in Canada this morning. Roads very bad the 7.30 morning bus arrived at Allendale at 11 o'clock.*
Sunday 19 Jan	*J Ridley, L Robson and I was over at Nenthead at night.*
Wednesday 22 Jan	*Got a wagon load of straw from M Harrison Silver Hill.*
Thursday 23 Jan	*Got 40 bales of oat straw from Allendale Farmers.*
Sunday 2 Feb	*It started to blast and within an hour the roads were blocked.*
Monday 3 Feb	*Blasted all day roads all blocked. Got 4 sheep out that had been overblown.*
Tuesday 4 Feb	*The blast has never stopped it has gone on since Sunday afternoon and still going on tonight.*
Wednesday 5 Feb	*The wind has gone down but it has snowed all day. Took 8 stone bundle of straw onto the fell with the milk barrow and a hard job we had.*
Thursday 6 Feb	*Still snowing but not so cold. They have just opened (the road) to Sparty Lea. Not started from Allendale end. Had no post since last Saturday.*
Friday 7 February	*A very cold day still snowing and blasting. Monday's mail came today. The main road not open yet. We have been sledging hay onto the fell all week.*
Saturday 8 Feb	*Still blasting this morning not snowing. No sign of a fresh. No roads open yet. Roads expected to open tomorrow between Allendale and Allenheads.*

MEMO	*Hay is going very fast. We have 1 yard deep in the pit barn and 1 half mue each in the barn. They are 2feet 6inches below the beams never been so short before. We have already bought 3½ tons of straw.*
Sunday 9 Feb	*Started to blast about 11 o'clock this morning and has been the worst of all. Was down to the Lead Mill Bridge with milk. I fear the roads will be blocked again.*
Monday 10 Feb	*Still blowing this morning. Roads all blocked in again. No mail, no milk away. Cannot get any hay to sheep with sled.*
Tuesday 11 Feb	*This has been another wintry day. Don't know when we will get any milk away. No mail since Friday. Nothing like any fresh yet.*
Wednesday 12 Feb	*Still blasting and snowing. The road just cut to the Peasmeadows. The roadman had to seek bread from Sinderhope. People up Dirt Pot taking hurt.*
Thursday 13 Feb	*70 men sought bread and other things from Sinderhope. The pressmen there and took photos of them. Road still blocked from the Peasmeadows to the Broadgate. Had mail today.*
Friday 14 Feb	*Men still carrying stuff from Sinderhope. A bulldozer on up to Sinderhope dykes. It is still very hard weather and a hard frost. A big report in the papers about Allenheads starving.*
Saturday 15 Feb	*Walked down to Sinderhope at night - my mother to go into RVI tomorrow. The roads still blocked from Elia to Sipton Bridge. A bulldozer and 100 men are on. No sign of any fresh yet.*
Sunday 16 Feb	*Was down at the Lead Mill Bridge with milk. Got a road through. First road since a fortnight today.*
Monday 17 Feb	*Men and bulldozer started at Lead Mill Bridge to come this way. Sheep having a hard time because it is so cold.*

Tuesday 18 Feb	*A road up past here. The bulldozer making a good job. Hay is getting very short. There will be a big loss this Spring.*
Wednesday 19 Feb	*Weather fair but very hard. Nothing like a fresh yet. Sheep are very keen of hay. Had the milk wagon first time since 22 Jan.*
Thursday 20 Feb	*Fair in the morning but started to snow again in the afternoon. Bulldozer came back off Whetstone Mea to the Lead Mill Bridge tonight.*
Friday 21 Feb	*It has blasted all day and all the roads are blocked in again. The 7.30 morning bus stuck at Sinderhope. The bulldozer cannot get on for the want of fuel and the wagon cannot get up to her.*
Saturday 22Feb	*Sheep are taking hurt now. We have 7 hoggs died this last day or two. The hay is getting very short - we have got one foot in the pit barn and two half mues in the other. Snow showers all day.*
Sunday 23 Feb	*Hoggs dying fast. Hard weather. Roads still blocked.*
Monday 24 Feb	*We got the sheep down Middlehope Lot and had a hard job. Gave them 8 sacks of hay and they cleared it all up. Everybody talking of hay getting short. Roads still blocked.*
Tuesday 25 Feb	*Main road opened at dinner time. The District men got to the Kiln Bridge. It started to blast at 10 o'clock at night. A very strong wind.*
Wednesday 26 Feb	*It has been a very rough night last night and blocked all the roads up again. It has blasted all day, the worst day of all and it is still raging tonight. Have not got Middlehope beast watered it was that rough.*
Thursday 27 Feb	*Better day not so much wind but snowing in the morning. Sheep are dying like flies. This is the worst winter in my time. No milk away since last Thursday.*

No mail since Monday.

Friday 28 Feb

Still snowing today nothing like a fresh. Roads still blocked.

Saturday 1 March

Fine day but very keen frost. Another 3 hoggs dead. The loss is terrible and no sign of any fresh yet.

MEMO

This has been the worst winter in my time of farming. We have lost somewhere about 20 odd sheep up till now and the hay is getting very short and only a little straw.

Sunday 2 March

Fine day hard frost. Nothing like a fresh yet. Down at the Lead Mill Bridge with the milk - had to go down by T Parker's and the Burnfoot.

Monday 3 March

The main road was cut through this morning.

Tuesday 4 March

Main road open but this one not. Only 4 snow cutters on and it (the road) is as full as I have ever seen it. The sheep are all over the place. I wish it would come a fresh. Ronnie came home from Canada today.

Wednesday 5 March

Looks like more snow. I hope not as the sheep are all over the place. Everybody is on about the hay.

Thursday 6 March

More snow through the night. Sheep dying 2, 3 and 4 in a day. Very disheartening time. Don't know what will happen in the Spring when the sheep turn heavy with lamb.

Friday 7 March

Started to blast this morning again. We are having a bad time. The hay is a severe problem. I fear the roads will be blocked tonight.

Saturday 8 March

Roads blocked. Was over in Middlehope cutting the dyke out to stop sheep coming home.

Sunday 9 March

Hard weather but fine. Sheep very hungry. Been on with sheep all day. No road up here yet. Hay is a very serious job.

Monday 10 March	*Blasting again last night - roads all blocked. Sheep dying every day. I have never seen anything like it.*
Tuesday 11 March	*Everybody shouting for hay - it can hardly be got.*
Wednesday 12 March	*It has come another blizzard tonight again. Digging a hole for dead sheep. We have dead all over the place, never had so much loss.*
Thursday 13 March	*Blasted all day. Roads all blocked again. This is the worst they have ever been. It is a terrible storm. Sheep are dying.*
Friday 14 March	*We have been burying sheep all day. Put 14 sheep into one hole and we have a lot more to bury yet. Snow cutters carrying bread from Allendale.*
Saturday 15 March	*Started to blast at dinner time and tonight is the worst I have ever seen. I have never seen things so bad as they are now. Tonight we have sheep in seven different place - they all have shelter but the weak ones lie down and are trampled on. It makes one frightened to look around in the morning.*
Sunday 16 March	*Last night was the worst night of all. I have never seen anything like it for blasting but by this morning it had gone to rain but it started to blast at night again.*
Monday 17 March	*Main road blocked the worst this winter. They have decided to cut a sled track down to Sinderhope and farmers are to go with sled to bring food stuff up.*
Tuesday 18 March	*Snowing and blasting again, roads all filled up again. We have had no mail for a week, no milk away since 8 March. 8 sheep dead this morning.*
Wednesday 19 March	*Snow cutters still carrying food stuff from Studdon. It has come softer but no sign of a fresh yet. Buried 14 sheep and many more to bury yet.*
Thursday 20 March	*Little bits of the hills bare, we have turned sheep onto the fell but the fresh not right yet. Buried 8 sheep.*

Friday 21 March	*It has come a good fresh today - rain and wind. Roads not open yet. H Heslop died at Morpeth and was brought by sled to Sinderhope and pulled by the snow cutters to Allenheads.*
Saturday 22 March	*Good fresh through the night. H Heslop buried. I was a bearer. He was pulled from Allenheads to St Peter's churchyard. The road at Dirt Pot was ankle deep in slush and water.*
MEMO	*We had the first mail on Friday 21 since Wednesday 12 March.*
Sunday 23 March	*Roads not open yet. Kenneth and me went down to Sinderhope to see my mother. She looked bright and talked all the time till we came away but we noticed a change just before we came away.*
Monday 24 March	*Roads opened this morning. Nixon's of Hammershield came to say they had had a phone message that my mother had had a very bad night. Blasting this morning.*
Tuesday 25 March	*Snowing. The snow cutter is on the Slag Hill. Hilda went down to Sinderhope. I went down with the bus at night and a change I saw in my mother.*
Wednesday 26 March	*Good fresh today. We cut the gate out and dug the car out. Went to Sinderhope at night, my mother very bad.*
Thursday 27 March	*Still fresh. Burying sheep every day and they are still dying. Went to Sinderhope at night, my mother did not know we were there. There is a big change.*
Friday 28 March	*Burying sheep all day. Hilda and I went to Sinderhope at night in the car. My mother sleeps all the time.*
Saturday 29 March	*Very misty night and roads narrow with snow.*
Sunday 30 March	*Got a phone message saying my mother died at 12 o'clock last night.*
Tuesday 1 April	*Went to Sinderhope and on to Hexham. Did not stay long came back to milk.*

Wednesday 2 April	*My mother was laid away today in St Peter's churchyard - a big funeral. Fair but still a lot of snow, had a job to turn the car at the Lead Mill Bridge.*
Thursday 3 April	*A cold day. Showers of sleet.*
Friday 4 April	*Sheep still dying every day. We have lost 90 up till now. Some have losses up to 500. The hay is a problem too everyboday is short and some out.*
Saturday 5 April	*Very cold nothing like an early Spring which everyone was looking for. I have never seen or heard tell of such a loss as there was this winter.*
MEMO	*I don't think we will ever forget this winter. Lorna born December 21 1946. My mother died March 30 1947 and the worst winter in living memory.*
Sunday 6 April	*This is the first real Sunday since 26 January. We went down to the churchyard at night and then on to Tedham. A very cold windy night.*
Monday 7 April	*Wet cold day. Burying sheep in the morning. Expecting hay coming - we are very short only ½ of a mue left.*
Tuesday 8 April	*Snowed all day and there 3-4 inches of snow on tonight. Hoping it will go soon. Got half a ton of hay from the Mill. They are giving everybody 10 bundles each. It is black stuff.*
Wednesday 9 April	*Snow is going.*
Friday 11 April	*Leading muck. The middens are full of snow.*
MEMO	*Allendale - Allenheads road only open 5 days in February this year. This has been the worst winter I have ever farmed in and the heaviest loss of sheep.*

There were very few entries in the diary until the end of the year.

The Snow Cutters Defy the '47 Drifts

Another casualty of the 1947 winter was Harrison Heslop. One of the many local men sporting a surname for a Christian name, Harrison lived in Dirtpot on the road between Sparty Lea and Allenheads.

He made a living for himself and his wife in many different ways. Primarily he was the Allenheads postman, his route covering the top end of Sparty Lea as far as Green Pitts. He was therefore John Joseph Varty's postman. When not out delivering mail, he mended clogs and boots for the miners, he sold paraffin and candles to heat and light the isolated cottages around his home and he worked a few acres on his smallholding to supplement his income.

In the early months of 1947 Harrison was taken to Hexham Hospital, middle aged and very ill. As the storm took hold of the hills he knew so well, Harrison passed away.

And then began another story in the book of human endeavour as his friends and neighbours drew together to bring his body back to Dirtpot. It was to be no mean task. Although a main road ran all the way up the valley, it was to be of no use being filled almost to the telegraph pole tops.

The Hexham hearse came as far as Allendale. Then the battle started. A local tractor turned out and led the body as far as Sinderhope where the snow drifts defeated even a tractor.

From Sinderhope local farmers and roadmen, who had been employed for 7/0d a day as snow cutters, left off from their work to pull the coffin on a sledge by hand over the fell tops of Sinderhope high above the blocked main road as far as Sipton.

At Sipton they met up with Dick Nichol, farmer and postman from Sparty Lea, who had managed to lead his horse up the fields. The horse took the burden from the men as far as Low Shield and on higher up the fellside past White Hill and further to the Coal Pitts where they were met by Fred Hutchinson from Allenheads with his sledge. Following the line of the main road way below them, the sad little party towed their friend to his home.

That night the storm relented enough for the funeral procession to bring Harrison Heslop to St Peter's churchyard the next day.

St Peter's Church – Sparty Lea

The following information is taken from an account of the Church written by the The Reverend B M Goodwins, Vicar of St Peter's from 1930-38.

The Rev William Maddison MA, former Vicar of St Peter's for 5½ years, penned the Foreword. He recalls the "warm hearted people of the Dale", the happy times he spent in their company and the reverence held deep in their hearts for the old Church.

With the aid of a grant of £100 from the Incorporated Church Building Society, St Peter's was enlarged in 1825. This resulted in an increased seating capacity for the congregation.

An old plaque used to hang on the west wall and read:

> This Chapel was Rebuilt and Enlarged
> in the year 1825, by which means 200
> additional sittings have been obtained
> and in consequence of a grant from the
> SOCIETY for promoting the Enlargement
> and Building of Churches and Chapels 180
> of that number are hereby declared
> to be free and unappropriated for ever
> and are in addition to 92 formerly provided.

> WILLIAM WALTON,   Churchwardens
> JOSEPH CURRY
> OLIVER DAWSON

It is not known what the former church building looked like but there is a record of repairs totalling £6-11-6d being made to St Peter's in 1670, indicating that the original building was of a much earlier date. Little of it remains except for the bell dated 1753 and possibly a tablet which used to hang on the North wall and read:

IN MEMORY
OF

THOMAS CRAWHALL
AGENT OF ALLENHEADS
WHO DIED AUGUST 8 1812
AGED 61 YEARS
AND OF

ANN CRAWHALL
HIS WIFE
WHO DIED SEPT 18 1822
AGED 72 YEARS

Probably an iron box in the Vestry also dated from the early Church. The Registers begin in 1807 but funerals took place from 1723 although those records were kept by the Parish Church of St Cuthbert in Allendale.

St Peter's was carved out of the main Parish in 1856. The building measured 28ft x 14ft and in 1823 Minister Walton describes its seating capacity as "for not more than 70 persons". The population of the High Forest Parish was 1,370. Indeed the whole of the Parish of Allendale did not exceed 4,630.

In 1823 it was decided to rebuild St Peter's Chapel the following year depending on a grant from the ICBS and from the rates of the Parish of Allendale. Mr Walton describes the population as being poor and mainly employed in lead mining.

The renovations totalled £460 and a grant from the ICBS was applied for on 14th February 1824. The grant application stated that in 1821 the population extended to 760 in the Chapelry of St Peter's (that included Allenheads) and baptisms and marriages were performed at St Peter's.

The provision of church room was for 70 at St Peter's. It was hoped to extend that to 200 allowing 4 1/2 ft per person.

The building was to be of stone and lime, 52ft x 24ft internal measurement and a height of 17ft 3in at the side walls. It was estimated that the cost including furnished fittings would be £460.

The Rev B M Goodwins faced a dilemma with the new seating arrangements for in 1825 Mr Walton had stated that there would be room for 270 persons.

St. Peter's Church beside the corn mill c.1900.

St. Peter's Vicarage stands at the roadside with the church, corn mill and River East Allen in the background. The footpath to Old Dyke can be seen in the field beyond.

However, in 1938, in the same building, there were only places for 121 rising to 150 if chairs were brought in. The only solution Mr Goodwins could arrive at was that Mr Walton had divided the entire floor space, i.e. altar, vestry, aisle, etc, by 4 1/2 - the space in feet allowed for each person. Indeed on 30th March 1824 Mr Walton wrote that they were not confined to any plan and, if necessary, they may even erect a small gallery to accommodate a larger congregation.

The first marriage to take place in the new church in 1825 was between John Ritson and Jane Dixon, neither of whom could sign their names. It is interesting to note here that in the mining bargain books for 1823 the vast majority of miners were able to sign their names clearly and confidently.

In 1827 Mr Walton himself was married in his new church to Jane Crawhall, daughter of William Crawhall, Mining Agent for Lord Allendale and surveyor for the new church. Mr Walton continued his Ministry at St Peter's until 1851.

From 1852 till 1878 the Rev Constantine O'Donel was Minister. In 1862 he moved from Allenheads to Sipton Shield, the Parsonage. We know that Mr O'Donel was an elegant gentleman, slender and tidy in silk hat and frock coat. His handwriting reflected his personality and the Registers from his time are a pleasure to read - Mr Goodwins says "a model for any schoolmaster".

His Irish blood had blessed him with a musical gift. Leading up to his departure from St Peter's in 1878 for Capheaton, he would ride there on his fell pony every Sunday to conduct the service and return to St Peter's for the service there.

The Rev James Maxwell Lister followed and in 1884 more repairs were carried out to the church at a cost of £70. Appearing in the Hexham Courant for 23rd February 1884:

> "Allenheads Church which has been closed for some time will be reopened on Friday evening, Feby 29th, the Revd Canon Barker of Hexham having kindly consented to preach at the opening Service. The collection will be in aid of the Church Expenses Fund."

In 1882 Mr Lister had the present Vicarage built so ending the use of Sipton Shield as a Parsonage. The new building earned the reputation of being one of the better situated and designed vicarages in the Deanery. It seems that during the building an old right of way was in dispute and caused much consternation. However, eventually the path was diverted to its present route following the south boundary of the property. The occupant of Old Dyke felt so strongly about the situation at the time that he put the problem into verse:

> "Now this Old Dyke's a sturdy tyke
> Who from the point won't stray
> But vindicates with all his might
> The people's right of way."

Mr Lister was succeeded in 1887 by the Rev W Williams from Yorkshire who stayed at St Peter's for 26 years. In 1892 he undertook to update the building as the North wall was bulging and unsafe. (This North wall proved to be a recurring problem because Mr Goodwins closed the church from October 1931 until September 1932 and held services in a wooden hut nearby in order that the wall, "far out of true", could be repaired.)

A Committee was set up to oversee the renovation and by February 1893 £240 had been promised. The total estimate was £650. Mr Williams was dubious that the plans could be executed in their entirety due to the poverty of the local people - most of them miners occupying no more than 3-10 acres.

Church attendance was reported to be good in summer and poor in winter owing to the cold conditions in the church rising from the stone flooring. It was hoped to put in a wooden floor. Other improvements included re-seating; replacing the ceiling with a hammer beam roof with tie rods; raising the chancel by one extra step. Repairs to the bell gable, the west windows and screen and the building of a small tower were to be delayed.

The church closed for a year during alterations during which time the contractor threw up his contract for two months. By November 1894 the work was completed to everyone's satisfaction.

In 1902 further improvements included a hot water apparatus, swing doors, coke and coal stores and repairing all side windows.

The Rev W Williams died on Christmas Day 1913 and his successor, the Rev D J B Lewis, had the centre South window filled with stained glass as a memorial to his predecessor's care for God's House.

More repairs followed in 1931 under the Ministry of the Rev B M Goodwins at a cost of £500 provided by Viscount Allendale. The South wall was underpinned and given a new foundation and the wall rebuilt to window levels. The roof was overhauled and a new boiler inserted and new oak half doors hung at the entrance.

On 11th September 1932 the church was reopened by the Lord Bishop of Newcastle and the Dowager Lady Allendale.

The walkway by St. Peter's Church beside the River East Allen

The group of locals who voluntarily tended the churchyard. This photo was taken
in 1978 to mark the successful restoration work.
Back row - ?, Arthur Graham, Raymond Archer, Louis Robson, Elsom Robson,
Cecil Noble.
Front row – Willie Parker, George Batey, John Heslop, George Nixon, Joe
Sparke, George Philipson.

St Peter's Churchyard

In 1890 the churchyard extended to ¾ acre. Additions appeared in 1895 and 1919. The oldest headstone which the Rev B M Goodwins could find dated from 1717 and was inscribed:

WILL LOWDON
Son of W:L:
Lived 5 days dy
ed December 5th
1717

Some of the following epitaphs are to be found in the old part of the churchyard:

1773
Thou art gone to the Grave
We will not deplore thee
Whose God was thy ransom
Thy guardian thy shield.
He gave thee He took thee
And death has no terror
The Saviour has died.

1779
All you that come to my grave to see
Like as I am so must you be
Fly sin therefore live godly still
Then welcome death come when it will.

1812
Like lilies drooping in their bloom
In prime of life I was cut down
Be careful therefore how you live
Death does not always warning give.

1846
Thou art gone to the grave,
Yet we cannot deplore thee;
Though sorrow and darkness encompass the tomb
Thy Saviour has passed through its portals before thee
And the light of His love is thy lamp through the tomb.

Between 1932 and 1938 over £120 was spent on paths, boundary walls, shrubs and trees. The riverside path was railed in and a lych gate erected at the riverside entrance in memory of the late Mr J W Metcalfe, Agent of Allenheads.

BAPTISMS:

In 1827 and 1830 children of parents who had been married at Gretna Green were christened at St Peter's

From 1807-62 there were 2,593 baptisms in the Church. From 1826-1937 there were 902 baptisms.

MARRIAGES:

Between 1825-1830 there were 63 marriages out of which 71 people could sign their names, the other 55 signed with a cross.

From 1837-1937 there were 507 weddings.

DEATHS:
Unhealthy mining conditions, poor medical attention and the rigorous climate probably accounted for the high mortality rate in the area in the 19th century.

MORTALITY RATES FOR YEARS 1832-35 AND 1932-35

1832-35 Pop. 1,736	Under 5 years	Under 25 years	Under 50 years	Over 50 years
	36	18	14	31
1932-35 Pop. 741	3	-	2	34

Only one person in the valley reached their century - Peter Green of Swinhope who died 9th June 1819 aged 100 years.

The first burial registered at St Peter's is for Thomas Medcalf of Elpheygreen 12th January 1813 aged 20 years.

Between	1813-1836	there were 793 burials
	1847-1901	there were 1,600 burials
	1901-1937	there were 435 burials.

It follows that some of the old ground must have been used more than once.

The last burial service in the church was for Thomas James Robson of Low Swinhope Shield on 17th March 1951.

OCCUPATIONS LISTED IN THE REGISTERS:

Vet Surgeon	Miller	Mining Engineer	Game Watcher
Smelter	Daysman	Husbandman	Yeoman
Roaster	Iron Stone Miner	Mail Contractor	Grocer
Clogger	Soldier		

LOCAL PLACE NAMES AS SPELT IN THE REGISTERS:

Sibton Shield	Cinderhope	Dirtpot	Kitley Rigg
Eleah House	Round Hill	Capel Show	Elphey Green
Foreside House	Scott's Meadows	Low Houses	"Black Horse Inn"
High Round Hill	High Town	Port Gate	High Dirtpot Shield
Tollbar Gate	Sligg Hill	Rope Half	Blacket's New Houses
High Sparty Lea	Burned House	Mount Pleasant	Gill Hill Cottage
Redburn Shield	Roan Tree Stob		

Entries from the Vestry Minute Book 1891-1915

Vestry Meeting for the Restoration of St Peter's Church held in the Vestry of St Peter's on Monday 23rd January 1893 at 6.30p.m.

It was unanimously agreed to carry out the recommendations of the Archdeacon Canon Cruddas, Mr Hicks and the Vicar:

1	Chancel roof and east window	£70
2	Nave roof and chancel arch	£110
3	Floors	£40
4	Seats	£50
		£270

Expenditure from Easter 1898 to Easter 1899:

Mrs Elliott cleaning	2 - 18 - 6
Mr Elliott clerk	2 - 15 - 0
P Spark collecting	1 - 0 - 0
Repairs of church	
& cottage	2 - 2 - 0
Mr G Philipson	
building wall	0 - 6 - 0
Mr Spark rcet	1 - 14 - 0
Mr J Philipson oil	0 - 6 - 0
Balance	1½
	11 - 3 - 1½

Mr Coulson ⎫
         ⎬ Churchwardens
Mr Craig ⎭

Mr Bailey   Board School master
                    occasional player on harmonium

Mr Yates   Lay reader

28 communicants

The Restoration of St Peter's Churchyard 1978

On the suggestion of the retired the Rev B M Goodwins, a Committee was formed with Mr Willie Parker as Chairman, Mr Elsom Robson as Secretary and Mr John Heslop as Treasurer.

In 13 days the dedicated band of workers, offering their individual skills, created a haven of peace out of the derelict wilderness that had once been the churchyard.

The following extracts are from a booklet which was produced at the time and details the work done.

The poem "Thank You", written by an unknown hand, describes "A Job Well Done".

Extracts from: THE RESTORATION OF THE BOUNDARY WALLS,
GATES AND BURIAL GROUND OF ST PETER'S,
SPARTY LEA DURING 1978

Prior to the work of restoration, the Burial Ground and its surrounding walls had presented a sorry sight. Now that this voluntary work has been accomplished the Committee hope that those families having graves of their dear ones in St Peter's will kindly keep them cared for and so assist in the maintenance of the Burial Ground.

The Committee, together with the Rector and Churchwardens, are especially grateful to the following:-

Mr and Mrs Wood of Corn Mill, for their kindness in providing building materials and the very welcome refreshments they provided throughout the restoration work. Also for the help of Misses Barbie and Fiona Wood.

Mr Raymond Archer and Mr Lloyd Fairless, for providing the tractors, trailers and building materials.

Mr Kenneth Graham, who made the gates in welded Sculpture.

Mr Herbert Robson, who made the wicket gate and the entrance gate.

And collectively to all the following:-

Messers. Willie Parker, George Philipson, Herbert Robson, Raymond Archer, Kenneth and Keith Graham, Arthur Graham, Stuart Beattie, George Batey, Joe Sparke, Dixon Nichol, John and Willie Martin, John Heslop, Peter Wood, George Nixon, Robert Grainger, Cecil Noble, Richard Robson, John Nixon, George Bell, Lloyd and Eddie Fairless and Elsom Robson.

This splendid body of men gave their spare time and energies to dry stone walling, the carrying of wall-filling materials from the river bed, cement mixing, footpath clearance, grass cutting and the trimming of trees and shrubs, and all other work necessary for the completion of the task they had set themselves.

Burial Ground Fund:

It was decided to set up a Fund to help pay for materials etc and we are grateful to those who subscribed. Due entirely to the voluntary service given by the afore-mentioned gentlemen, this money has now been banked by the Committee and will be used as and when necessary for the upkeep of the Burial Ground.

Service of Thanksgiving for the Restoration:

The Service of Thanksgiving was held on Wednesday 30 August and was attended by a large number of friends. The newly appointed Rector conducted the Service and the Rev B M Goodwins, a former Vicar of St Peter's Church, preached a Sermon.

This Service was a twofold Thanksgiving, firstly for the Restoration of the Burial Ground and secondly for the spirit of fellowship and self-giving that inspired the completion of the restoration.

Our thanks also to their Minister, the Rev Kenneth Coates, for kindly choosing the hymns for the Service and allowing us to use their hymn books. And indeed to Mrs Edith Philipson for her musical accompaniment.

It was a most memorable occasion, a work well done. To each one who took part in this restoration we again offer our sincere thanks.

R W Parker, Chairman.
J P Heslop, Hon. Treasurer.
J H E Robson, Hon. Secretary

Sparty Lea Methodist Chapel prior to it being moved a few yards south, in 1914, to the present position.

Sparty Lea Chapel as it stands today.

The Chapel

At Sparty Lea and Swinhope
At Tedham and Allenheads
There were four Chapels all thriving
In the heyday of the lead.

The strength of Wesley's preaching
Found a home in the Dalers' hearts
Encouraged by the Company
Methodism grew in these parts.

Sparty Lea moved up the hill.
Now an active congregation
An ardent, happy Sunday school
For the younger generation.

Swinhope's doors are closed now,
Built in 1845
Scene of the famous miners' speech
"For a better deal we must strive."

Allenheads with gleaming woodwork
Nestles under Killhope Law
The bazaar with goods and lovely teas
Attracts young and old from near and far.

Tedham Chapel near to Sipton
Has long since disappeared.
By those who worked the mighty wheel
The Lord's name was there revered.

Gone or standing empty
Or reverberating His Glory
The Chapels of the upper dale
Are a part of the miners' history.

Jennifer Norderhaug
1987

Sparty Lea Chapel

Sparty Lea Chapel was rebuilt in 1914. Nicholas Glendinning undertook the building work while John Reed from Hope Head and Henry Robson from Old Dyke (Reed and Robson) did the joinery work and Thomas Dodd, blacksmith from Allenheads made door bands and lamp hangers.

The former Chapel was taken down at a cost of £5.

The following items are taken from the account book for the Chapel and give an indication of prices during the First World War and in the 1920s. The dedication of a zealous population in the activities for their Chapel is also evident.

Between July and December 1914 almost £600 was paid out to builders, joiners, solicitors etc for work on the new Chapel. In the month of November six services were held and the collections realized £43-6-2½d, a notable amount for the time and for a village population.

In 1915 these are some of the expenditures listed:

Jan	Mr C Stephenson, Hexham (Plumber)	£14 - 16 - 2
	Newman Bros, Hexham (Plaster work)	£35 - 0 - 0
	Joseph Graham, Allenheads (10 days work)	£ 2 - 0 - 0
Feb	John Little for carting stones	18 - 0
	St Peter's Education Committee	£ 1 - 1 - 0
	C W S (new lamps)	£ 6 - 5 - 0
Apr	Allendale Store (floor covering)	£ 4 - 5 - 0
Sept	W R Temperley (tiles and cement)	£ 1 - 5 - 11

1917 some expenditures include:

Jan	John Philipson (supper & Expenses 3 dates)	11 - 2
	Fire Insurance	14 - 0
	Orphanage	2 - 0
	Legal Defence	1 - 0
	Aged Local Preachers	1 - 0
Mar	Printing Hand Bills	3 - 6
	W Liddell (coals & coke)	11 - 9
	J Parker (bag of coke)	1 - 3
	Mrs Hewitson (chapel cleaning)	15 - 0
May	Rowell & Sons (hot water pipe repairs)	£20 - 8 - 9

| June | Door mat for porch | 5 - 3 |
| July | Mrs Hewitson (chapel cleaning) | 15 - 0 |

Dec   Income from the Silver Tree = £20 - 5 - 0
             Income from   Seat Rents = £ 1 - 1 - 0

In 1918 a charge of 6/6d was paid for a Tune Book for the organ; 10/0d for lamp oil and £1-5-0d for larch posts and rails for fence while a concert party by Kidds of Wearhead brought in £2-15-4d and another by the Hudson's party netted £7-6-0d. The Minister at that time was the Rev Wm Armstrong.

In 1919 income included:

May	Greenside Quartette Party	£ 5 - 0 - 7½
June	Gift Sale & Supper	£26 - 15 - 0
July	T Hollands Concert	£ 1 - 10 - 11½
Nov	Greenside Quartette Party	£ 7 - 19 - 9½
Dec	Silver Tree collection & supper	£23 - 7 - 6

Expenditure included many transport hire charges:

Feb	Trap hire for Hudson Party	£ 1 - 0 - 0
Mar	J Shields motor to Haydon Bridge	£ 1 - 8 - 0
May	Trap hire for Quartette	£ 1 - 8 - 0
Aug	T Holland & family lodging	£ 1 - 4 - 0
Oct	Greenside Party expenses	£ 2 - 0 - 0
Dec	John Shield Motor to Haydon Bridge & Catton	£ 1 - 10 - 0
	John Shield Motor to Allendale	9 - 0
also	T Pigg (1lb butter)	2 - 6
	Groceries for 2 efforts	5 - 9
	John Charlton (½lb butter)	1 - 3
	J V Hill (10 galls oil)	18 - 0
	Wm Liddle (cart of coke)	15 - 4
	Joseph Parker (cart of coke)	£ 1 - 5 - 4

In 1920 Sparty Lea Chapel began to hire the bailer from J Varty at 3/6d per time.

1923 - A Sale of Work was held in St Peter's School and a total of £83-8-2d was raised; the hire of the school cost 17/6d.
The bailer charge had risen to 4/6d.
The Rev Palmer was the Minister and Mrs Peart was the caretaker with F Sparke in charge of lighting and heating.

1925 - Mrs Renwick took over as caretaker and received £7-6-0d for her year's wages.

1926 - Sale of Work brought in £77-15-7d and a winter concert was given by Allenheads Christian Endeavour.

1927 - The organ was cleaned at a charge of £1 paid for by a donation. It was noted that butter had dropped to 1/8d per pound.

1929 - A new organ was purchased for £32. The old one was advertised (1/0d for the advert) but there is no record of it having been sold until 1947 when a Mr Tom Philipson of Sparty Lea Terrace bought the Chapel organ for 5/0d.

1930 - Mrs Fred Sparke is new Chapel cleaner. Rev Pinchen is new Minister.

1931 - The Beacon Lights from Catton gave the Silver Tree concert.

1932 - Thomas Watkin is the Minister. £1-7-6d paid to C Stevenson (plumber) for casting the boiler.

1933 - Silver Tree concert given by Mrs Nevin Reed's concert party. 3/2d paid to Allendale Coop for new lamp glasses.

1934 - Silver Tree concert given by Harry Pigg's party from Keenley. Mr Batey's concert party from Allendale gave the Harvest Festival concert. Sale of fruit gave £1-0-0d.

1935 - Bill for provisions:

10 galls paraffin	=	6/8d
5 lamp glasses	=	2/1d
4 wicks	=	1/6d
Butter & coffee	=	1/9d
Years coke (2 tons)	=	£2 - 5 - 0d
Coal (2 bags)	=	3/0d

1936 - Minister was Rev S F Pawson

1937 - 2 dozen teaspoons bought for 6/0d

1938 - £5-5-9d paid to L B Fairlamb for a boiler.
Rev Wm Atkinson is new Minister.

1942 - Rev Welch arrived.

1944 - Paid L B Fairlamb £28-14-0d for a new boiler.

1945 - Minister was Thos J Evans. Paid Mr H C Robson £1-11-1d for puttying and painting windows which he returned to the Chapel. Paid £14-15-0d for 70 sheets of asbestos wood (Turnall) including cartage & postage.

1948 - 20 new hymn books bought for the Chapel at a cost of £4.

1949 - Mrs Wanne new cleaner. Paid Jack Elsom £1 for repairing the road.

1950 - Paid Joseph Sparke £29-3-0d for building porch.

1951 - Paid £62-0-0d to R A Wilkinson for completion of porch.

1952 - Sale of Swinhope Chapel for £120-0-0d.

1954 - Bought 2 electric fires for £18-11-0d.

1955 - Miss Liddle gave an organ to the Chapel - paid J M Ridley £1-10-0d for delivery. £1-10-0d taxi fare from St John's to Sparty Lea for concert party.

1958 - Donations received for the use of the schoolroom for funeral parties from the Noble family for their mother's funeral and from Dick Nichol for his wife's funeral. Paid Harris Engineering Co £118-8-0d for installation of gas heating.

The last entry in the old Trust Treasurer's book is for June 1963:
Bring and Buy Sale income £57-12-8d.

Swinhope Methodist Chapel 1845-1968

The following items are taken from the Accounts books from the Chapel kindly loaned by Miss Annie Featherstone of Sparty Lea.

The preface to the first book reads:

Bought of Mr Barkas Nov 20 1845

30 Watts Songs	2 - 1d
20 First class books	1 - 7d
50 Second " "	3 - 10d
50 Third " "	5 - 7d
Specimen catechisms	10d
3 Question books First class	4½d
4 " " Second class	6d
1 " " Third class	4d
1 Bible testament	1 - 6d
Paid	16 - 7½d

The accounts for 1845/46 were examined and audited by John Hopkinson.

In the midst of all the troubles at the Allenheads Lead Mine in 1849 the following entry appears in the Accounts book:

1849   May 13   Presents for the Swinhope Sunday School Scholars which is gone for Americk   Presented by the teachers

7 Bibles	5 - 10d
3 Testaments	1 - 0d

Income for the Chapel in 1853 included payments by these people:

Jane Milburn	1 Hymbook	2 - 0d
Rebeckah Ball	1 Hymbook	2 - 0d
Jane Whitfield	1 Himbook	2 - 0d
Jane Jackson	1 Himbook	2 - 0d
Isabella Nattrass	1 Himbook	2 - 0d
Thomas Reed	1 Himbook	2 - 0d
Jane Milburn	1 Testament	4d
E Roddham	1 Testament	4d

Robert Armstrong	1 Testament	4d
Mary Peart	A donation	6d
Ann Charlton	1 bible	6d
Roseina Collson	1 bible	4d

Sunday School Anniversaries preached by W H Thompson and T Dargue.

In 1895 and 1898 two mentions are made of a Trip to Tynemouth, the first amounting to 16-6d and the second to 14-7d. The trip appears to have been for the Sunday School.

No accounts seem to have been kept from 1938-40 and only scant entries after that. From 1956 only Silver Tree Expenses are recorded and the final entry is for September 1968 £1-0-0d for Silver Tree Expenses.

Swinhope Methodist Chapel in 1987. In 1849, four years after opening, it was the meeting place for the striking lead miners and Joseph Heslop's memorable tirade against "blacklegs".

Swinhope Chapel and Allenheads Lead Mine Strike 1849

New regulations at the Allenheads Mine, stating that the agents would appoint "watchers" to check the miners' working hours and that the working day was to entail eight successive hours of work, caused a General Strike by miners and the strike lasted for 18 weeks from January until the beginning of May.

Meetings took place all over the valley and delegates were appointed to present the miners' case before the Chief Agent, Mr Atkinson. They also tried to meet with Mr T W Beaumont at Bretton Park, their employer's Yorkshire seat, but he was desperately ill at that time.

At one such meeting on March 21 in the Swinhope Methodist Chapel the following speech was made, possibly by Joseph Heslop. The strength of feeling against the "blacklegs" is evident and even frightening:

"In the first place I want you all to know that you have liberty to go to work when you think proper. You have it in your power to either keep your old masters or to have a whole set of new ones. This I can assure you from the best authority. I have a letter in my pocket which I am not prepared at present to let you all see or else you would take courage anew and cry with one voice 'the day is ours'. Now lads, my orders out of this pulpit to this meeting is that every man has liberty to begin work, but it is my hope and earnest prayer that if any man do begin work in connection with them that has begun, that you will have the goodness to pass by them and their wives and families without speaking to them, to have no connexion or communication with them. If they are sick do not visit them; if they are in need of a doctor do not ask them one; if they die do not bury them; if they are fastened underground in the mines do not assist in seeking them out but let them die, or be killed in the dark, and go from darkness to darkness into the fury of the devil to be kept by him without remorse in the fire of Hell for ever and ever. You are all to torment them while on earth and when they die may the devil torment them to all eternity. Let them be like Judas, only fit for taking their own lives if none of you do it for them. And if they emigrate to Australia or America if any of you should be there be sure to treat them in the same way. For I can tell you for one that if I had a houseful of bread and every other necessary of life to take and to spare I would not give one of them a mouthful to save their lives if I saw them dying of want in scores and I hope you will follow my example."

This speech was delivered under a wall-hanging reading "God is Love".

Strong letters were written to the press blaming the Head Mining Agent, Thomas Sopwith, and his under agents William and John Curry.

Eventually Mr Sopwith brought 30 men in from Alston to work the mine. Retaliations against this move met with 100 men being told they would never again be employed at Allenheads.

And so the strike came to an end - the miners defeated, misled by their delegates who were also discharged. The cost of the action to Mr Beaumont amounted to £9,000 and many families were left destitute.

On May 17 1849, 60 people left East Allendale to start a new life in Illinois, USA.

This was the only strike ever to take place at Allenheads mine.

Swinhope mill cottages near to Swinhope Chapel.

St Peter's School, Sparty Lea

THE EARLY DAYS

There existed a school at St Peter's on the east side of the Church as early as 1825, the site being known as Chapel House. One of the first schoolmasters was Hugh Shield at the time when the Rev William Walton was Curate of St Peter's Church.

Hugh Shield had previously been schoolmaster at Low Coalcleugh, being paid approximately £10 per annum for his labours.

At the same time the Curates of West Allen High and St Peter's Chapels, up to and probably long after 1835, used to give tuition to the miners' children. They were paid 1/6d per quarter plus an annual payment of 5 shillings from certain categories of miners and 2/6d from other categories.

Later in the 1840s and onwards the schoolmaster of St Peter's was John Heslop. He was paid £8 per year by W B Beaumont and there would be around 60 pupils in his care. Mr Heslop was incapacitated with a wooden leg and had the nickname of "peg leg Heslop".

Then Thomas Sopwith came to the Dale. Both he and his employer, Mr W B Beaumont were deeply interested in the education in the area. Sopwith wrote: "The liberality of Mr W B Beaumont in building and supporting good schools is beyond all praise."

In January 1877, 200 ratepayers met to discuss the formation of a school board for the parish. The motion was carried and election of members was by ballot. The Board first met in April of the same year and Allenheads, Sinderhope, Keenley, Carrshield and Ninebanks schools were transferred to the Board while it was agreed to build new schools at Allendale Town and Catton and at St Peter's to replace the old school by the Church.

The new school was built in 1879 between Old Dyke and Coatenhill Dam. There was one large schoolroom and one smaller room for the infants.

In 1886 the members of the School Board were:
Mr Thomas Elliott (Chairman), the Rev John Gill, Messrs William Pigg, Thomas Ritson, Lancelot Bell, Ridley Robinson, Caleb Hetherington, John Henderson, William Thirlwell, William Ridley and William Temperley. Mr Bell Dixon was the Clerk.

The original St Peter's School was situated on the Church Bank directly below and within sight of the new school building, completed in 1879 and opened in 1880.

After 37 years as teacher at the old school, how sad that Mr Heslop missed the completion of the new school by only one year.

St. Peter's School was built as a Board School in 1879 and opened in 1880. In 1975 it was converted into a private house after the school was closed in 1973.

St. Peter's School Pupils c.1920s
(as recalled by Annie Featherstone)

Back row (left to right) – Maurice Liddell (Lot Head), John Liddell (Waterhouses), John Liddell (Lot Head), Alec McVay (Tilery cottage), Fred & Willie Robson, Willie Graham (Huntwell), 2x? Philipson (Tedham)

2nd from back row – Ella Wilson, Elspeth Philipson (Swinhope), Ethel Rowell, Lucy Walker, Elsie Reed (Hope Head), Lily Parker (Burnfoot), Molly Graham (Huntwell), Barbara Noble (Swinhope Mill).

2nd from front row – Laurence Reed, ? Philipson (Tedham Green), Tom Featherstone, ? Wilkinson, Herbert Robson, Leslie Noble (Swinhope Mill), John Whitfield.

Front row – Margaret Wilson, Annie Featherstone, Beatrice Nixon, Mary Featherstone, Jennie Parker, Mary Kidd, Winnie Kerno.

St. Peter's School, Sparty Lea c.1920s

Back row – Left to right -Teacher: Thomas Matthew Bell,
John Liddle (Lot Head), ?, John Liddle, ?, Mary Nixon, Elspeth Philipson,
William Liddle.

Front row - ? Williamson, Molly Pigg, ? Renwick, Eva Reed, Annie
Featherstone, Ella Wilson, Barbara Bell.

Extract from One of St Peter's Board School Log Books

St Peter's Board School, Sparty Lea was built in 1879 on its new site by the Old Dyke.

Mr W Sparke was Chairman of the Board.

The Water Rate from the Allendale Estates was 5/0d per half year paid annually on 11th November.

The Master of the new school was Mr A Sowerby.

August 23 1880	School opened with 37 pupils
Aug 30 1880	The role had increased to 49 pupils
Sept 3 1880	The role stood at 50 pupils
13 Nov 1880	Mrs Sowerby was appointed Sewing Mistress
26 Nov 1880	Installation of the school fires - found to be smoking. The school is cold.
	Ruth Reed was appointed School Monitor on a month's probation.
Feb 4 1881	Prize giving and Concert Day
March 3 1881	20feet snow drifts at the gate of the school
March 25 1881	Difficulty in obtaining ages of pupils, parents won't or can't fill in the declaration forms
May 6 1881	Allendale Town Fair
	Vandalism to the school building - broken windows
May 30 1881	Examination candidates: Standard - 21 boys, 34 girls
	Infants - 6 boys, 1 girl
	Clerk - L C Lockhart
May 12 1882	School closed due to smoking chimneys, doors were opened but this exposed the children to draughts.
June 30 1882	Half yearly pay day at Allenheads. End of the school year. Mr Metcalfe Head of Sinderhope School.
July 3 1882	No register so names entered in log book. Entered names at 9a.m. attendances marked at 9.50a.m.

1st Class:	H Philipson	Mgt E Philipson
	Matt Milburn	Frances Liddle
	James Robson	Cath Elliott
	Robt Coulson	Chris Robson

Thos Varty
Jared Winter
John Bell
John Armstrong
Jos Ellison

May A Reed
Hannah MacMillan
Isab. Milburn
Mgt Philipson
Jane Robson
Emily Pigg
May Dodd

2nd Class:

Jno W Elliott
Jno Reed
Naaman Philipson
Thos Noble
Gilbert Graham
Jno W Robson
Thos Reed
Jno W Graham
Jno R Eliott
Thos C Armstrong
Jos P Reed

Perthemia Philipson
May Wilson
May Reed
Emma Robson
Mgt Liddle
Ann Metcalfe
May Milburn
Sarah Dodd
Mgt Milburn
May Noble
Mary Whitfield
Mgt Whitfield
Sarah Philipson
Mary Reed
Mary Buglass

3rd Class:

Thos Rowell
Will Robson
Jno Jos Lowery
Jno Liddle
Jno Lee
Jno Philipson
Jno Reed
Thos Buglass
Nicholas Reed
Thos Robson
Jno Reed
Jos Reed
Matt Liddle
Joseph Milburn
Jos Armstrong
Thos Stokoe

Mary Maughan
Mgt Milburn
Hannah Milburn
Elizabeth Liddle
Sarah Liddle
Mary Hewitson
Anne Curry
Harriet Dodd
Jane Wilson
Isab. Ellison
Jane Reed
Mary Curry
R J Maughan
Ellen Milburn

Sept 1 1882	Sports Day in field lent by Mr Sparke. Prize: cricket bat and ball. Children then marched back to school for buns, teacake etc. After tea more games then prizes for Regularity of Attendance and Government Examination.
Sept 14 1882	School closed - Mill Show. Elizabeth Philipson prepared for local examination.
Sept 29 1882	Home tuition - Government requires that a female be present during tuition in the home of a Master.

HER MAJESTY'S INSPECTORS' REPORT 1882:

Exceedingly good examination in the 3 elementary subjects. Reading good with intelligence and good modulation. Good diction. Composition fair. Handwriting good. Arithmetic good. Order exceedingly good. Needlework excellently good. Grammar fairly good - some uncertainty about moods and voices of verbs in the higher standards. Geography fair. No payment made for M Coulson.

L Lockhart - Clerk

Oct 6 1882	School gates worn - no framework and wood wearing on stone. School roof requires attention. Fires still smoking.
Dec 8 1882	15 feet snow drifts. No school all week. Closed early for Christmas holidays. The storm continues.
Feb 16 1883	Richard II reader for Standard VI and VII Song - "Far Away"
May 30 1883	Teacher absent with rheumatic fever. (Absent until June 22.)
May 31 1883	Mrs Reed taking over. School closed until June 15 due to Measles epidemic.
June 22 1883	Smoke cap on classroom chimney needs attention. Notice received of annual HMI visit for July 10. Number of children eligible for examination: Above 7 years - 23 boys, 32 girls. Under 7 years - 5 boys, 7 girls. Children ineligible for examination: Over 7 years - Nil. Under 7 years - 3 girls. Total on register - 70 pupils.
July 10 1883	HMI inspected school (P Pennelthorne) Master - Matt H Sowerby Pupil Teacher - Mgt Coulson, Head of 2nd year.
July 17 1883	Hay Harvest. School closed for Midsummer 19 July.

Aug 24 1883	School reopened. Hay not finished.
Sept 22 1883	School closed for the Mill Show.
Sept 28 1883	School bell out of repair.
Oct 26 1883	Hannah MacMillan prepared for Pupil Teacher examination. Elizabeth Philipson (former PT) now gone to Carr Shield school.
Nov 30 1883	Writing to and visiting parents about bad attendance.
Jan 11 1884	Teacher presented with a fine fat duck, a pair of kid gloves and a neck kerchief as a mark of respect.
April 10 1884	Mr Williams - Head of Sinderhope School.
May 9 1884	Margaret Coulson, Pupil Teacher, about to resign her position.
May 16 1884	The number of pupils on the register numbered more than 70. Teacher expected to instruct all the pupils this week without assistance - increasingly difficult due to the large number of pupils never having been to school before and on reaching 7 years have to acquire 3 years work in 9 months prior to the examination. Children without exeption have made consecutive progress from Standard to Standard. This makes it impossible for one teacher to devote sufficient time to the remaining Standards.
May 23 1884	Mental arithmetic taught to all Standards with most unsatisfactory results.
May 30 1884	Average attendance 68.3.
June 20 1884	Informed by Mr Spark that Hannah McMillan has been appointed temporary monitor in place of Margaret Coulson. Board decided that the globe requisitioned was unnecessary and could not be granted.
June 27 1884	Mr Dickinson instructed one of the pauper children to leave school owing to the child having reached the age for which the guardians ceased to pay. Teacher used his influence for the child to continue until the time of examination.
July 4 1884	Great difficulty in getting children ready for the exam in Standard V. Difficult to get them to attend owing to it being their object to discontinue school whether they pass the exam or not.
Aug 22 1884	School reopened one week ago. Teacher resigned his position as master having obtained an appointment in Newcastle.

Corporal Punishment:
In all cases of corporal punishment the fact of the administration to be recorded in the log book. Corporal punishment to be

inflicted only by means of the tawse and only in extreme cases of misdemeanour.

Home Lessons:
No child to receive any home task or lesson under 10 years of age and no child, in any way delicate, to receive any home lesson during its school course over and above 10 years of age.

Aug 26 1884	Attempted to have the footbridge completed which the teacher, by great endeavour, succeeded in having constructed over the river for the benefit of Tedham, Ellershope, Sparty Lea and other children on their way to school.
Sept 12 1884	I this day resign my position as Master of this school. Signed: M H Sowerby.
Sept 15 1884	I this day commenced duties as temporary Master of this school. Signed: Thomas Bowerbank.
Friday ??	Annual Sheep Fair held at the Corn Mill - according to custom the school had holiday. It is the greatest day of the year.
Nov Friday ?	During the 8 weeks I have been here the children have been remarkably punctual, regular and docile so have had no occasion to resort to corporal punishment. T B.
Nov 10 1884	I commenced duties as Master of this school this 10th day of November 1884. Signed: W S Cambridge.

Standard IV backward in arithmetic, Writing good. 1st, 2nd and 3rd Standards backward in all these subjects. Owing to there being no books ordered for this year I find it very difficult to carry out the timetable.

Nov 17 1884	Changed girls' sewing class time as previously it was too dark after the sewing to get any other work done.
Nov 24 1884	Arrival of Readers for this year's work. Commenced to give lessons to Pupil Teacher Hannah McMillan in the presence of my wife.
Dec 2 1884	Attendance very much reduced owing to the severity of the weather.
Dec 24 1884	Hannah McMillan still absent through sickness. Children presented me with a fine leg of mutton and Mrs Cambridge with a beautiful shawl and brooch as a token of respect together with a very nice letter wishing us the compliments of the season.
Jan 12 1885	Reopened school with 48 children. Weather very rough. Hannah McMillan recommenced her duties.

Jan 19 1885	Report for Her Majesty's Inspectors for 1884:

Reading (accuracy and fluency) - fairly good
Modulation of the voice confined to a few children in the Upper
Standards; some lack of distinct enunciation.
Intelligence in subject matter - fair
Spelling: Standard 1 - 4 - fair
Composition - barely fair
Handwriting - fairly good
Arithmetic: Standard 1 - 7 - fair
Mental Arithmetic: Standards 1-7 - fair
               "   4   - good
Repitition - correct
Grammar - good
Geography - good
Singing - good
Order - good

Signed: B Dixon (Clerk).

Feb 14 1885	Very much annoyed with chimneys smoking - have had to keep doors open but children feel the drafts. School almost unbearable during westerly winds.
Mar 5 1885	Half the children in lower Standards absent due to the severe snow.
Mar 20 1885	Smoke and soot falling. 1st class register got rather wet owing to rain dripping through the roof.
May 8 1885	Half the children came to school and asked for leave of absence due to parents attending the Cattle Fair. Close the school.
May 20 1885	Laura Bright, Standard 11, died yesterday.
July 6 1885	13 children absent this morning owing to the peat season.
July 17 1885	Owing to the backward state of the hay harvest a number of children are still employed helping their parents in the fields. Have decided to extend the holiday another week.
July 24 1885	Reopened school with 68 children.
Sept 18 1885	Holiday - Corn Mill Cattle Show.

Report for Her Majesty's Inspectors for 1885

The school has suffered from two changes of teachers and the results are very fair. The order is good. A good map of the country and a clock are needed.

Oct 2 1885   Attendance is not what I desire. Out of 77 children on the books the average is 69.

Nov 9 1885   Received the first complaint on school method since I came - the party declining to allow her child to do homework.

Dec 24 1885   Presented with a couple of ducks and Mrs Cambridge with two pairs of ornaments. Sewing Mistress and Pupil Teacher presented with a beautiful silver brooch.

Jan 11 1886   Reopened school with 20 scholars. Presented the children with oranges, apples and sweets.

Jan 18 1886   Great quantity of snow - had to dig yard gates out to get an entrance to the building. School closed at 3.20p.m. to give children a chance to get home before dark.

Feb 2 1886   According to accounts from the oldest inhabitants there has been no such snow storm for 60 years.

Feb 8 1886   Have been compelled to close school 20 times since 19 January. Some children have not been at school since before Christmas.

Feb 15 1886   Drifts of snow 8 feet in places.

Mar 3 1886   No abatement of the storm. It has snowed incessantly for 30 hours. The drifts are 10-15 feet high.

Mar 9 1886   The storm has abated. The snow is still uncut on the roads leading to the school.

NB *At the end of the last century the very position of the Schoolmaster depended upon the pupils' achieving good results in the annual examination. These results, together with the Inspector's Report on the school, decided whether the Master could retain his position for another year. The local Vicar, the Board of Governors or the Inspector could demand the resignation of the teacher if they felt standards were not being upheld. It was absolutely essential then that the Master ensured regular attendance for continuity of learning.*

J.N.

Mr Holgreaves, Master of St Peter's

The following snippet comes from Mr Lawrence Graham, formerly of the Allen Valley and presently living in Queensland, Australia.

He recalls the family of Grahams from Huntwell and in particular the incident in 1937 when Tom Graham, his son Eddie and a band of chaps, built the stone wall next to Water House at Sparty Lea.

Mr Holgreaves, then retired as Master of the school, came most days to watch the "old boys" of St Peter's complete the task.

Lawrence Graham writes:

"They did the Sparty Lea road junction in about 1937. It was a big project in those days and many of the men working on it were old boys of St Peter's.

Their retired school master came most days to inspect the work and talk to his old boys.

As a mark of respect for him they made a cement block with his name and the year on it and the Grahams built it in to the wall.

On the day it was laid Mr Holgreaves went to the bank in Allendale, came back with a pocket full of half crowns and when they put the stone in place, he climbed on the half built wall and made a speech saying how much he appreciated what they were doing, also how much they all meant to his life, then he gave each of the workmen a new half crown."

The stone still stands in the wall at the corner of Water House but the shale from the bank has fallen away over the years and covered the inscription stone. In 1986 Raymond Archer from Tedham tried to uncover the writing and it may be possible to move it to a more prominent position.

It reads:

A L HOLGREAVES
APRIL 1939

Thomas Matthew Bell - Headmaster of St Peter's School 1926-1944

A chapter on St Peter's School could not go by without mentioning one of the most remembered and notable Head Teachers in its history - Mr Thomas Matthew Bell, nicknamed "Chappie"

Almost from the first day we moved into the school we heard tales of the famous Mr Bell. After a while it felt as though we walk the school with him, such was his influence on the building, the gardens and the local people who, 40 years after he taught them, speak of him as though he might pop his head around the door at any moment.

He was the epitome of the strict but fair old-fashioned teacher. No nonsense, sharp punishment but ready to reward hard work, able to share a joke and with a passion for wildlife, flowers and gardening.

The School Garden was famous in its day thanks to Thomas Matthew Bell. He created a vegetable patch in which the lads had to take their turn. St Peter's is on a very exposed site at just on 1,000ft and Mr Bell's own son, Thomas Matthew, was able to tell us that the best shelter from the wind was just over the school wall where the vegetable patch had been. When sent out by his father to take a turn in the garden, he would opt for the vegetables and spent many an hour hiding behind the wall - out of the classroom and out of the wind!

But Mr Bell's horticultural speciality was his rockeries. His widow says that wherever they moved to, they had to build a rockery. And massive and impressive structures they were.

The rockery at St Peter's is much diminished now but a fair section of it remains. Hard , heavy boulder clay forms the centre and stones carried by the lads - who remember it well - from the nearby Elpha Green quarry decorate the top. In its heyday St Peter's rockery housed more than 200 different alpine plants. However, it's not the plants which the elderly men of the valley remember so much as the carting of the heavy stones up the steep hill from the quarry! The late Cecil Noble used to recall also carrying sand from the bottom of the drained Coatenhill Dam to mix in with the soil for some of the rare plants.

Maurice Reed, now Auctioneer and Valuer for Hexham Auction Mart, worked like a beaver in the garden during his time at St Peter's. Apparently Mr Bell would "reward" pupils who had finished their school tasks and worked hard in the classroom by allowing them an afternoon in the open air on garden work. On one end of year report Maurice received the dubious compliment: "Maurice should do well, he is a good gardener."

Stories of school days fill the school even now when local folk come to visit and it is never long before Mr Bell's name is heard.

Raymond Archer recalls being asked by Mr Bell if he had ever climbed to the bell. When Raymond answered that he had not, Mr Bell seemed to look surprised as though he had not expected Raymond to be afraid of such a trick. So some time later Raymond decided to please Mr Bell by doing the climb. When Mr Bell came storming out of the school to see who was ringing the school bell, Raymond eagerly owned up - and got the cane!

It was the tradition at Christmas for pupils to give the teacher a present. One Christmas, on the day of breaking up, a child brought a goose into school for Mr Bell and his family. A lovely present - the only problem was that it was still alive and Mr Bell, his wife and two children were to drive to Scotland to spend the festive holiday with Mrs Bell's parents in Largs. The only solution was to put the squawking goose into the dicky seat at the back of the old car. Later that evening, relieved to be released, the goose was presented to an extremely surprised mother-in-law.

Another Christmas, kindly, one of the lads in the woodwork class offered to make a wheelbarrow for young Thomas' Christmas present. A beautiful barrow was carefully made and painted and the lad wheeled the new present to Peasmeadows, where the Bells were living, to be hidden for Christmas morning. When the young Thomas saw the barrow he was delighted, then his little face fell and he complained, "Santa has been using this wheelbarrow - look the wheel's all dirty."

In 1987 I met Mr Bell's son, Thomas, and his widow, now an elderly lady in her 80s but with a fond memory of St Peter's. Mr Bell had moved from St Peter's in 1944 to take up a post at Whitley Chapel School in Hexhamshire and then he retired and spent many years in Peebles following his favourite hobby gardening and botany before his death in the 70s.

I asked Mrs Bell, now living outside of Newcastle, if she would like to see the old school again. She arrived one summer afternoon, the sun shining and the wind howling in true Sparty Lea fashion. As she put her finger on the door bell, a pane of glass blew out of the little schoolroom window and lay shattered in a thousand pieces over the carpet. Still stunned by the crash, I opened the door, wished her welcome and led her along the school hall to show her what had happened. She smiled gently and said, "Well it's 44 years since I stepped through that door so someone here must be saying - 'oh, not those Bells again!'"

Whether it was somebody or just the wind making a statement, it was a joy to hear her reminisce, to watch her pointing out where the stage had been for the many concerts, to be allowed to share her brief visit into her past. This is our home now but we are happy to share it with and privileged to walk the school with "those Bells".

Tom Bell, a former pupil at St. Peter's School.

Tom Bell's Schoolboy Memories

The following extract comes from an article featured in the Hexham Courant in 1982. It was written by Tom Bell of Cornwall and part of a larger work describing his childhood in Sparty Lea. A copy of the original manuscript was given to me during my time in St Peter's School. Twenty years later in 2008 his family have published a book based on Tom's reminiscences. This extract covers some of his schoolday memories with the headmaster Thomas Mattew Bell.

Classroom

The school was one large room with a little annexe for the infants, who were taught by the headmaster's only assistant, Miss Stokoe. The head - nicknamed "Chappie" by the children - had to cope alone with all the classes from standard one onwards.

The high windows of the gaunt classroom let in hardly any sunshine. We sat in groups of four at heavy oak desks with cast iron ends. The walls were painted a dirty cream and were devoid of any decoration, apart from a large map of the world with the British Empire in red, and a picture of Jesus with a flaxen beard.

The school served an area for miles around, ranging from the farms on the very edge of the fell on the Killhope side to the top end of Swinhope at Hope Head and down to the farms at Tedham Green and Sipton.

We left at 14 years of age - except for the lucky ones such as myself who had a birthday during a holiday and could leave at 13.
The school had no musical instrument, and for music lessons the whole school sang together. Chappie began by humming the note from a tuning fork and asking us to hum it too (the various noises that came out were unbelievable) and next he would hum a few bars and get us to join in.

Mischievous

I loved these lessons. Songs like "The Farmer's Boys", "Shenandoah" and "Hearts of Oak" were the only poetry and music in our lives, and for me the only real enjoyment in school.
Otherwise, the four terms I spent at St Peter's were largely wasted. We senior boys were bored most of the time and were mischievous to alleviate the boredom. There was no physical education of any kind, no organised games and no art, craft or science lessons.

We senior boys sat at the far end of the room at the back; the furthest from authority but also the furthest away from the only source of comfort in winter - the stove.

During the bitterly cold days we were too dispirited even to get into mischief. The stone would be stoked up to its maximum heat with part of its iron chimney glowing red, but only a few yards away the cold was almost unbearable; we could hardly hold a pen or a slate pencil and had to do exercises such as astride jumping and thigh-slapping to warm up.

On the frequent wet days we were allowed to drape our soaked jackets and coats over the fireguard. As the clothes steamed, smells of byres and barns, stables and sheepfolds were released and spread throughout the bleak classroom like an earthy incense.

My last term at St Peter's was my happiest. Chappie began to teach us bookbinding, and Bill and I settled down to the job and enjoyed it.

We had all the gear - stitching frame, needles, glue pot, strawboard, bookbinder's cloth, a vice, a wooden mallet and woodchisels for trimming edges. When we finished our first volume of Harmsworth's encyclopaedia in green cloth with black corners we were very proud.

Autumn term came to an end. We leavers shook hands with Chappie and said goodbye. But going home along the Swinhope Lonnen on this dark and gloomy day before Christmas, the day I'd looked forward to for so long, I did not experience the happiness I'd expected.

Read more about Tom's reminiscences in the following book -
"A Ha'penny over the High Level, a Tyneside and Northumberland childhood"
by Thomas Knowles Bell. Illustrated by Tony Kenyon.
Published by Tyne Bridge Publishing. ISBN:978-185795-118-9. £6.99

Head teacher Mrs. Marjorie Davison and her seven pupils. They are, left to right, David Fairless, aged eight, Robin Archer, eight, Hazel Archer, six, Beryl Archer, five, Margaret Field, six, Derek Fairless, six, and Paul Borrowdale.

Parents call for school closure

By Journal Reporter

PARENTS in a lonely Northumberland valley have asked that their local school be closed — 11 years after they fought to keep it open.

The change of heart over the future of Allendale St. Peter's Primary School at Sparty Lea follows a decline in the number of children in the Swinhope Valley.

The one-teacher school now has only seven pupils, aged between five and eight.

And there is only one child of pre-school age in the valley.

Three parents, who account for six of the seven pupils, now want their youngsters transferred to Allendale Primary School eight miles away down the East Allan Valley.

They say it has more facilities and the children would be with more of their own age.

Last night, Mr. Raymond Archer, of Tedham, said: "It would be easier for our kiddies, certainly in winter, to travel on the bus to Allendale."

A report, to be presented to Northumberland Education Committee, recommends closure.

If the committee accept, it is planned to close the school next Easter.

CENSUS YEAR: 1851 For the Parish of the High Forest Grieveship

Name of House	Name and Surname	Relation to Head of Family	Age M	Age F	Rank, Profession or Occupation
Scotch Meadows	John Liddle	Head	31		Lead Ore Miner
	Elizabeth Liddle	Wife		31	
	Thomas Liddle	Son	10		Scholar
	Mary Liddle	Daughter		9	Scholar
	John Liddle	Son	1		
Scotch Meadows	Matthew Rowell	Head	35		Lead Ore Miner
	Jane Rowell	Wife		32	
	Margaret Rowell	Daughter		10	Scholar
Scotch Meadows	Jane Roddham	Head Widow		55	Householder
	William Roddham	Son	19		Lead Ore Miner
	Christopher Roddham	Son	17		Labourer
Scotch Meadows	Christopher Philipson	Head	41		Lead Ore Miner
	Mary Philipson	Wife		32	
	John Philipson	Son	9		Scholar
	Margaret Philipson	Daughter		8	
	Jane Philipson	Daughter		4	
	Rebecca Philipson	Daughter		2	
	Nicholas Philipson	Son			
Low Scotch Meadows	Sarah Roddham	Head Widow		63	Householder
	Matthew Roddham	Son	25		Lead Ore Miner
	James Roddham	Son	23		Lead Ore Miner
	Thompson Roddham	Son	19		Labourer
	Christopher Roddham	Son	16		Lead Ore Dresser
	Jane Roddham				
Hammershields	William Coats	Head	23		Lead Ore Miner
	Sarah Coats	Wife		22	
	Hannah Coats	Daughter		1	
Hammershields	John Elliott	Head	29		Lead Ore Miner
	Margaret Elliott	Wife		31	
	George Elliott	Son	6		Scholar
	Nevin Elliott	Son	5		
	Ann Elliott	Daughter		2	
	Mary Sparke	Visitor		31	Dressmaker

Place	Name	Relation	Age (M)	Age (F)	Occupation
	Ann Sparke	Visitor	8		Scholar
Middlehope Green	Joseph Milburn	Head	59		Mason
	Watson Milburn	Son	20		Mason
	Mary Milburn	Daughter		22	
	John Milburn	Son	17		Mason
	Elizabeth Milburn	Visitor		29	
	William Milburn	Visitor	2		
	Sarah Milburn	Visitor		1	
Coal Pit House	William Hewitson	Head	26		Surgeon & General Practitioner
	John Thompson	Visitor	64		Surgeon & GP
	Mary Routledge	Servant		28	House Servant
Byrehope	Thomas Dickinson	Head	36		Lead Ore Miner
	Ann Dickinson	Wife		26	
	John Dickinson	Son	5		
	Mary Dickinson	Daughter		2	
	Jane Reed	Servant		24	General Servant
Byrehope	Joseph Curry	Head Widower	67		Quarryman
	John Curry	Son	38		Lead Ore Miner
	Frances Curry	Son's Wife		33	
	Margaret Curry	Daughter		9	Scholar
	Ann Curry	Daughter		7	Scholar
	George Curry	Son	5		
	Henry Curry	Son	1		
	Jane Dickinson	Daughter Widow		35	Pauper
	Henry Dickinson	Son	13		Lead Ore Miner
	Ann Dickinson	Daughter		11	Pauper
	Margaret Dickinson	Daughter		9	Scholar Pauper
Byrehope	Hugh Nixon	Head Widower	57		Lead Ore Miner
	Robert Hewitson	Son in law	26		Lead Ore Miner
Byrehope	Francis Hewitson	Head	31		Lead Ore Miner
	Sarah Hewitson	Wife		26	
	Ann Hewitson	Daughter		6	
	Mary Hewitson	Daughter		4	
	Hannah Hewitson	Daughter		2	
	Sarah Hewitson	Daughter		7m	
Byrehope	Ann Currey	Head Widow		34	
	Matthew Currey	Son	11		Lead Ore Washer
	Joseph Currey	Son	7		
	Ruth Currey	Daughter		4	
	Thomas Currey	Son	1		
Elia	Francis Philipson	Head	70		Lead Ore Washer
	Jane Philipson	Wife		65	

	John Philipson	Son	25		Lead Ore Washer
	Jane Philipson	Grand daughter		7	Scholar
	Jane Sparke	Servant		16	House Servant
Elia	John Stobbs	Head	41		Lead Ore Miner
	Elizabeth Stobbs	Wife		36	
	Dickenson Stobbs	Son	11		Scholar
	Mary Stobbs	Daughter		4	
White Hill	John Philipson	Head	54		Lead Ore Miner
	Mary Ann Philipson	Wife		25	
	Ester Philipson	Daughter		6	
	John Philipson	Son	4		
	Harry Philipson	Son	4m		
	Jane Philipson	Daughter		16	
Low Shield Close	George Stokoe	Head	76		Blacksmith
	Sarah Stokoe	Wife		72	
	Margaret Stokoe	Daughter Spinster		55	
	John Stokoe	Grandson	22		Blacksmith
Ellershope	Sarah Pattinson	Head Widow		60	
	Thomas Pattinson	Son	38		Lead Ore Miner
	Jane Telford	Servant		18	General Servant
Ellershope	John Charlton	Head	36		Lead Ore Miner
	Jane Charlton	Wife		38	
	Mary Charlton	Daughter		7	
	Henry Charlton	Son	6		
	Thomas Charlton	Son	4		
	Hannah Charlton	Daughter		1	
Ellershope	Thomas Curry	Head Widower	55		Lead Ore Miner
	Ann Curry	Daughter		24	
	Elizabeth Curry	Daughter		18	
	John Vickers	Son	15		
	Joseph Vickers	Grandson	2		
Ellershope	Shield Reed	Head	41		Lead Ore Miner
	Jane Reed	Wife		39	
	Thomas Reed	Son	18		Lead Ore Miner
	Jane Reed	Daughter		11	Scholar
	Mathilda Reed	Daughter		4	
	William Sparke	Visitor	4		
	Joseph Gibson	Son in law	23		Lead Ore Miner
	Mary Gibson	Wife		21	
	Jane Gibson	Daughter		1	
Ellershope	William Johnson	Head	51		Miner
	Jane Johnson	Wife		45	
	Anthony Johnson	Son	21		Lead Ore Miner

Place	Name	Relation	Age (M)	Age (F)	Occupation
Ellershope	William Gibson	Head	41		Cla & Paten Maker
	Mary Gibson	Wife		42	
	William Gibson	Son	20		Lead Ore Miner
	Errington Gibson	Son	17		Lead Ore Miner
	Hannah Gibson	Daughter		15	
	Mary Gibson	Daughter		13	
	John Gibson	Son	10		
	Jeffery Gibson	Son	8		
	Ann Gibson	Daughter		4	
	Jane Gibson	Daughter		2	
Ellershope	Miles Maughan	Head	57		Retired Miner
	Mary Maughan	Wife		52	
	Jacob Maughan	Son	24		Lead Ore Miner
	Hannah Maughan	Daughter		17	
	Miles Maughan	Son	15		Lead Ore Miner
	Thomas Maughan	Son	10		Lead Ore Washer
Ellershope	Joseph Philipson	Head	51		Lead Ore Miner
	Phillis Philipson	Wife		44	
	John Philipson	Son	20		Lead Ore Miner
	Matthew Philipson	Son	16		Lead Ore Miner
	Martha Philipson	Daughter		14	
	Joseph Philipson	Son	11		Lead Ore Washer
	Mary Philipson	Daughter		5	Scholar
	Francis Philipson	Son	2		
	John Richardson	Son in law			
	Hannah Waugh	Servant		14	
	Thomas Richardson	Visitor	32		Lead Ore Miner
Shield Close	John Varty	Head	44		Lead Ore Miner
	Ann Varty	Wife		45	
	John Varty	Son	18		Lead Ore Miner
	Matthew Varty	Son	16		Lead Ore Washer
Hill Side	John Glenwright	Head	31		Miller
	Mary Glenwright	Wife		25	
	George Glenwright	Son	3		
	Hannah Reed	Servant		20	House Servant
	Elizabeth Robson	Mother in law		62	Proprietor of house & land
Hill Side	Jacob Dawson	Head	39		Lead Ore Washer
	Mary Dawson	Wife		35	
	Joseph Dawson	Brother	30		Lead Ore Miner
High Sparty Lea	John Stobbs	Head	29		Lead Ore Miner
	Jane Stobbs	Wife		24	
	Hannah Stobbs	Daughter		4	
	Christopher Stobbs	Son	1		
	Michael Stobbs	Brother	25		Lead Ore Miner

Place	Name	Relation	Age (M)	Age (F)	Occupation
High Sparty Lea	John Reed	Head	42		Lead Ore Miner
	Mary Reed	Wife		43	
	Isaac Reed	Son	19		Lead Ore Miner
	? Reed	Son	15		Lead Ore Washer
	John Reed	Son	10		Scholar
	Matthew Reed	Son			Scholar
	Hannah Reed	Daughter		5	
	Ann Reed	Daughter		2	
Tedham	Matthew Philipson	Head	45		Lead Ore Miner
	Rebekah Philipson	Wife		45	
	Thomas Philipson	Son	19		Lead Ore Miner
	Forster Philipson	Son	17		Lead Ore Miner
	Joseph Philipson	Son	14		Lead Ore Miner
	John Philipson	Son	11		Scholar
	Andrew Philipson	Son	6		
	Matthew Philipson	Son	2m		
	Mary Jackson	Servant		15	General Servant
Sparty Lea Gate	Matthew Martin	Head	74		Toll Bar Keeper
	Elizabeth Martin	Wife		69	
	Matthew Clark	Grandson	20		Labourer
	Matthew Dickenson	Grandson	8		Scholar
Tedham	Joseph Rowell	Head	40		Lead Ore Miner
	Mary Rowell	Wife		38	
	Ann Rowell	Daughter		7	Scholar
	Edward Rowell	Son	6		Scholar
	Joseph Rowell	Son	2		
Tedham	Oliver Whitfield	Head	38		Lead Ore Miner
	Elizabeth Whitfield	Wife		28	
	Margaret Whitfield	Daughter		2	
	Joseph Whitfield	Son	1		
Tedham	George Chatt	Head Widower	57		Lead Ore Roaster
	William Chatt		20		Labourer
	Elizabeth Chatt			18	
Tedham	Hannah Rowell	Head Widow		47	Pauper
	Margaret Rowell	Daughter		18	
	Wilkinson Rowell	Son	14		Lead Ore Washer
	Thomas Rowell	Son	12		Lead Ore Washer
	William Rowell	Son	10		Lead Ore Washer
	Joseph Rowell	Son	1		
Sipton Cottage	Thomas Dickenson	Head	24		Lead Ore Silver Separator
	Frances Dickenson	Wife		25	
	John Dickenson	Son	5m		
	James Robson	Visitor	56		Retired Miner
Tedham Green	Joshua Thirlwell	Head	27		Lead Ore Smelter

	Margaret Thirlwell	Wife		27	
	Ann Thirlwell	Daughter		9	Scholar
	Mary Ann Thirlwell	Daughter		3	
	Isabel Thirlwell	Daughter		2	
Tedham Green	John Reed	Head	24		Lead Ore Miner
	Mary Reed	Wife		21	
Tedham Green	Thomas Reed	Head	48		Lead Ore Miner
	Lydia Reed	Wife		49	
	Thomas Reed	Son	20		Lead Ore Miner
	Joseph Reed	Son	17		Lead Ore Miner
	Mary Reed	Daughter		14	
	Jane Reed	Daughter		12	
	Joseph Milburn	Grandson	4		
Sparty Lea	Joseph Sparke	Head	45		Lead Ore Miner
	Mary Sparke	Wife		43	
	John Sparke	Son	14		Lead Ore Washer
	Isabella Sparke	Daughter		18	
	Thomas Sparke	Son	9		Scholar
	Joseph Sparke	Son	5		
	Hannah Sparke	Daughter		2	
Sparty Lea	William Whitfield	Head	34		Lead Ore Miner
	Jane Whitfield	Wife		33	
	Elizabeth Whitfield	Daughter		2	
	Margaret Whitfield	Daughter		1	
Sparty Lea	William Robson	Head	48		Stone Mason
	Hannah Robson	Wife		51	
	William Sparke	Son in law	30		Land Surveyor
	John Sparke	Son in law	28		Stone Mason
	Ann Robson	Daughter		21	
	George Robson	Son	19		Stone Mason
	Thomas Robson	Son	17		Stone Mason
	Henry Robson	Son	15		Stone Mason
	Hannah Robson	Daughter		12	
	Jane Robson	Daughter		9	
	Elizabeth Dent	Niece		24	
Sparty Lea	George Philipson	Head	41		Lead Ore Washer
	Margaret Philipson	Wife		41	
	Hannah Philipson	Daughter		17	
	Jane Philipson	Daughter		15	
	Sarah Philipson	Daughter		15	
	Joseph Philipson	Son	10		
	Margaret Philipson	Daughter		8	
	Ann Philipson	Daughter		7	
	George Philipson	Son	2		
	John Philipson	Son	8m		
Sparty Lea	Robert Archer	Head	26		Lead Ore Miner

Place	Name	Relation	Age (M)	Age (F)	Occupation
	Mary Archer	Wife		21	
Sparty Lea	William Elliott	Head	25		Lead Ore Miner
	Jane Elliott	Wife		22	
	John Elliott	Son	2		
Water House	John Dickenson	Head	52		Lead Ore Smelter
	Isobella Dickenson	Wife		51	
	Robert Dickenson	Son	20		Lead & Silver Separator
	Hannah Dickenson	Daughter		18	Dressmaker
	Elizabeth Dickenson	Daughter		14	
	Jane Dickenson	Daughter		12	Scholar
	William Dickenson	Son	10		Scholar
Ellershope Shield	William Burnip	Head Unmarried	42		Cartman
	Leah Burnip	Sister Unmarried		38	
	Mary Burnip	Daughter		13	
	William Reed	Visitor	26		Cartman
Ellershope Shield	Ann Vickers	Head Widow		49	
	Thomas Vickers	Son	22		Lead Ore Miner
	George Vickers	Son	20		Lead Ore Miner
	Frances Vickers	Daughter		15	
	Joseph Vickers	Brother	53		Lead Ore Miner
St Peter's Chapel House	John Heslop	Head	41		School Master
	Mary Heslop	Wife		40	
	Thomas Heslop	Son	13		Scholar
	John Heslop	Son	9		Scholar
	Joseph Heslop	Son	7		Scholar
	Mary Heslop	Daughter		2	
Side House	Henry Philipson	Head Unmarried	46		Farmer of 75 acres
	Hannah Green	Servant		43	House Servant
	Mary Stokoe	Servant		16	Farm Servant
	George Philipson	Nephew	23		Miller
Round Hill Field	Elizabeth Sparke	Head Widow		46	Pauper
	Ann Sparke	Daughter		14	
	Thomas Sparke	Son	12		Lead Ore Washer
	Elizabeth Sparke	Daughter		9	Pauper Scholar
	Margaret Pears	Nurse Child		6	Pauper
Breckon Hill House	William Watson	Head	46		Lead Ore Miner
	Mary Watson	Wife		45	
	William Watson	Son	21		Lead Ore Miner
	Mary Watson	Daughter		17	
	Robert Watson	Son	14		Lead Ore Washer
	Dorothy Watson	Daughter		11	

	Joseph Watson	Son	8		Scholar
	Henry Watson	Son	6		Scholar
	Rhoda Watson	Daughter		4	
	Hannah Watson	Daughter		2	
	William Waugh	Wife's brother	47		Lead Ore Miner
Peasmeadows	James Richardson	Head	74		Grocer
	Hannah Richardson	Wife		67	
	Ann Heslop	Servant		37	General Servant
Peasmeadows	John Varty	Head	47		Lead Ore Miner
	Elenor Varty	Wife		57	
	Sarah Varty	Daughter		14	Scholar
Peasmeadows	John French	Head	27		Lead Ore Miner
	Hannah French	Wife		28	
	Joshua Philipson	Son	8		
	Hannah Philipson	Daughter		7	Scholar
	Matthew Philipson	Son	5		Scholar
	William French	Son	2		
Peasmeadows	John Dickenson	Head	25		Lead & Silver Separator
	Mary Dickenson	Wife		32	
	Isabella Dickenson	Daughter		4	
	Ann Dickenson	Daughter		1	
Peasmeadows	John Dargue	Head	57		Lead Ore Miner
	Hannah Dargue	Wife		57	
	Mary Dargue	Daughter		33	
	John Dargue	Son	26		Lead Ore Miner
	Jacob Dargue	Son	21		Lead Ore Miner
	Harrison Dargue	Son	17		Pupil Teacher
Peasmeadows	Jane Rodham	Head Widow		52	
	Mary Rodham	Daughter		24	Dressmaker
	John Rodham	Son	22		Lead Ore Miner
	Mary Hodgeson	Visitor		22	
Peasmeadows	Mary Lee	Head Widow		70	
	Matthew Lee	Son	47		Quarryman
	Nicholas Lee	Son	30		Game Keeper
	Elizabeth Lee	Daughter		34	
Peasmeadows	John Bright	Head	47		Lead Ore Miner
	Hannah Bright	Wife		52	
	Joseph Bright	Son	20		Lead Ore Miner
	Hannah Bright	Daughter		17	
	John Bright	Son	16		Lead Ore Washer
	Richard Bright	Son	13		Lead Ore Washer
	Thomas Bright	Son	11		Scholar
Peasmeadows	Thomas Heslop	Head	33		Lead Ore Miner

	Elizabeth Heslop	Wife		27	
	Isobella Heslop	Daughter		7	Scholar
	John Heslop	Son	5		
	Archbold Heslop	Son	4		
	Elizabeth Heslop	Daughter		2	
	Hannah Heslop	Daughter		5m	
Peasmeadows	John Lowery	Head Widower	57		Lead Ore Smelter
	Hannah Lowery	Daughter		28	
	William Lowery	Son	23		Lead & Silver Separator
	Margaret Lowery	Daughter		17	
	John Lowery	Grandson	8		Scholar
	Sarah Lowery	Granddaughter		8	Scholar
Peasmeadows	William Walton	Head	50		Smelting Agent
	Mary Walton	Wife		52	
	Margaret Walton	Daughter		21	
	William Walton	Son	18		Surveyor
	Isobella Walton	Daughter		16	
	Joseph Walton	Son	14		Scholar
	Edward Walton	Son	14		Scholar
	Mary Walton	Daughter		11	Scholar
	Joseph Carr	Servant	18		General Servant
	Ann Robinson	Servant		18	House Servant
Elia	James Philipson	Head	38		Lead Ore Miner
	Jane Philipson	Wife		41	
	Jane Philipson	Daughter		11	Scholar
	James Philipson	Son	6		Scholar
	Francis Philipson	Son	4		Scholar
	John Philipson	Son	1		
	Thomas Irwin	Nephew's son	4m		
Guide Post	John Whitfield	Head	71		Retired Miner
	Mary Whitfield	Wife		58	
	Dawson Whitfield	Son	21		Lead Ore Miner
	Joseph Whitfield	Son	17		Lead Ore Miner
	Jane Whitfield	Daughter		10	
	John Reed	Lodger	2		
Guide Post	Thomas Renwick	Head	31		Lead Ore Miner
	Elizabeth Renwick	Wife		26	
	Ann Renwick	Daughter		2	
	Joseph Renwick	Son	10m		
	Thomas Robson	Lodger	21		
Guide Post	Hannah Peart	Head Widow		54	Miner's Widow
	Jane Peart	Daughter		28	
	John Peart	Son	24		Labourer
	Henry Peart	Son	20		Lead Ore Miner
	Christopher Peart	Son	17		Lead Ore Miner
	Archbold Peart	Son	15		Lead Ore Washer

Guide Post	John Hewitson	Head	29		Lead Ore Miner
	Ann Hewitson	Wife		25	
	William Hewitson	Son	4		
	Emmerson Hewitson	Son	3		
Shaw House	Robert McMillan	Head	31		Lead Ore Miner
	Emmerson McMillan	Brother	28		Lead Ore Miner
	Elizabeth McMillan	Sister		26	
	Sarah McMillan	Sister		17	
Swinhope Edge House	Joseph Midcalf	Head	45		Lead Ore Miner
	Elizabeth Midcalf	Wife		33	
	John Midcalf	Son	14		Scholar
	Ann Midcalf	Daughter		12	
	Joseph Midcalf	Son	11		Scholar
	Thomas Midcalf	Son	9		Scholar
	Moses Midcalf	Son	5		
	Aron Midcalf	Son	2		
	Sarah Midcalf	Daughter		1	
Shaw House	Joseph McMillan	Head	31		Lead Ore Miner
	Jane McMillan	Sister		20	
	Maria McMillan	Sister		16	
Mount Pleasant	Matthew Varty	Head	39		Lead Ore Miner
	Elizabeth Varty	Wife		31	
	Matthew Varty	Son	8		
	Mary Varty	Daughter		5	
	John Varty	Son	3		
	Elizabeth Varty	Daughter		3	
	Rebekah Jane Varty	Daughter		4m	
Green Pitt	Mary Varty	Head Widow		63	Miner's widow
	Elizabeth Varty	Daughter		27	House Servant
	Thomas Varty	Son	25		Lead Ore Miner
	Joseph Varty	Son	22		Lead Ore Miner
Gaping Goose	Elizabeth Philipson	Head Widow		71	Miner's widow
	Nicholas Philipson	Son	47		Lead Ore Miner
	Matthew Philipson	Godson	4		
	Elizabeth Philipson	Goddaughter		1	
Gaping Goose	Ann Bell	Head Widow		32	Miner's widow
	Thomas Bell	Son	11		
	Mary Bell	Daughter		8	
	Martin Bell	Son	6		
	Robert Bell	Son	3		
	Ann Coulterd	Visitor		56	
	Robert Wilkinson	Lodger			

White Rigg	Thomas Coulson	Head	37		Lead Ore Miner
	Maria Coulson	Wife		51	
	Robert Chatt	Son in law	16		
	James Chatt	Son in law	43		Lead Ore Washer
	David Coulson	Son	11		Scholar
	Rosina Coulson	Daughter		9	
White Rigg	John Wilkinson	Head	48		Lead Ore Miner
	Jane Wilkinson	Wife		44	
	John Wilkinson	Son	25		Lead Ore Miner
	Ann Wilkinson	Daughter		21	
	Adam Wilkinson	Son	19		Lead Ore Miner
	William Wilkinson	Son	16		Lead Ore Miner
	Hugh Wilkinson	Son	14		Lead Ore Miner
	Job Wilkinson	Son	12		Lead Ore Washer
	Paul Wilkinson	Son	9		Scholar
	Cain Wilkinson	Son	7		Scholar
	Mary Wilkinson	Daughter		4	
	Jane Wilkinson	Daughter		1	
Stripe House	John Noble	Head	58		Lead Ore Miner
	Margaret Noble	Wife		58	
	Richard Noble	Son	20		
	Andrew Noble	Son	11		Shepherd
Stripe House	George McMillan	Head	51		Lead Ore Miner
	Mary McMillan	Wife		52	
	George McMillan	Son	21		
	Emmerson McMillan	Son	19		
	Harrison McMillan	Son	17		
	Mary Ann McMillan	Daughter		4	
	Elizabeth Curry	Servant		14	General Servant
High Moss House	John Wilson	Head	33		Lead Ore Miner
	Richard Ward	Brother	27		Lead Ore Miner
	Mary Ward	Sister		31	
Moss House	Elizabeth Peart	Head Widow		56	Miner's widow
	Mary Peart	Daughter		30	
	John Peart	Son	26		
	Hannah Peart	Daughter		21	
	Watson Peart	Son	18		
	Elizabeth Peart	Daughter		15	
	Adam Peart	Grandson	7		Scholar
	William Peart	Grandson	3		
Pasture Nook	George Milburn	Head	39		Grocer
	Jane Milburn	Wife		46	
	Jane Milburn	Daughter		11	
	William Milburn	Son	9		

			Age (M)	Age (F)	
	Margaret Milburn	Daughter		5	
	Mary Ann Milburn	Daughter		3	
	Ellenor Milburn	Daughter		1	
	John Coulson	Son in law	22		Lead Ore Miner
	Robert Coulson	Son in law	19		Labourer
	Ruth Coulson	Daughter		17	
Hope Head	Thomas Whitfield	Head	43		Lead Ore Miner
	Jane Whitfield	Wife		50	
	Thomas Dickinson	Son	12		Lead Ore Washer
	Ann Gibson	Lodger		5	
Hope Head	John Reed	Head	29		Lead Ore Miner
	Hannah Reed	Wife		28	
	Joseph Reed	Son	3		
	George Reed	Son	2		
	Thomas Reed	Son	1m		
	William Reed	Brother	25		Unemployed
	Mary Whitfield	Servant		16	House Servant
Hope Head	Robert McMillan	Head	26		Lead Ore Miner
	Mary McMillan	Wife		23	
	Thomas McMillan	Son	1		
Hope Head	Ann Bell	Head Widow		37	Miner's Widow
	Thomas Bell	Son	16		Lead Ore Miner
	Rebekah Bell	Daughter		8	
Hope Head	John Reed	Head	47		Lead Ore Miner
	Jane Reed	Wife		42	
	John Reed	Son	14		Lead Ore Miner
	Walton Reed	Son	9		Shepherd
	Jane Reed	Daughter		5	
	Margaret Reed	Mother		72	Miner's widow
Pry House	John Milburn	Head	31		Lead Ore Miner
	Elizabeth Milburn	Wife		31	
	Margaret Milburn	Daughter		5	
	Robert Milburn	Son	3		
	William Milburn	Son	1		
Pry House	Isaac Rodham	Head	22		Labourer
	Isabella Rodham	Wife		20	
	Ann Rodham	Daughter		1	
Pry House	John Midcalf	Head	51		Lead Ore Miner
	Mary Midcalf	Wife		36	
	Richard Midcalf	Son	4		
	Jane Midcalf	Daughter		2	
Pry House	Matthew Wilkinson	Head	23		Lead Ore Miner
	Elizabeth Wilkinson	Wife		29	

Place	Name	Relation	Age (M)	Age (F)	Occupation
Pry House	Teasdale Whitfield	Head Widower	75		Retired Miner
	John Whitfield	Son	37		Lead Ore Miner
	Mary Thirlwell	Servant		22	House Servant
Intack Head	Jane Hull	Head Widow		54	Miner's widow
	John Hull	Son	35		Lead Ore Miner
	Matthew Hull	Son	33		Iron Miner
	Robert Hull	Son	29		Iron Miner
	Isaac Hull	Son	26		Shepherd
	Robert Hull	Son	25		Lead Ore Miner
	William Hull	Son	22		Iron Miner
	Jesse Hull	Son	20		Iron Miner
	Thomas Hull	Son	17		Lead Ore Miner
	Ann Hull	Daughter		12	Scholar
	Phillis Whitfield	Daughter Widow		31	Miner's widow
	Jane Whitfield	Granddaughter		5	Scholar
	William Whitfield	Grandson	9		Scholar
	Mary Waggott	Servant		19	House Servant
Black Cleugh	John Reed	Head	62		Lead Ore Washer
	Phillis Reed	Wife		64	
	Mary Ann Reed	Daughter		27	
	Edward Reed	Son	24		Lead Ore Miner
	Robson Reed	Son	22		Lead Ore Miner
Black Cleugh	Wilkinson Nattrass	Head	43		Lead Ore Miner
	Mary Nattrass	Wife		36	
	Thomas Nattrass	Son	15		
	Isabella Nattrass	Daughter		8	
	John Nattrass	Son	6		
	Margaret Nattrass	Daughter		2	
Hay Rake	Joseph Reed	Head	54		Retired Miner
	Elizabeth Reed	Wife		48	
	William Reed	Son	20		Lead Ore Miner
	John Reed	Son	18		Lead Ore Miner
	Pattinson Reed	Son	6		
	Joseph Reed	Son	10		
Hay Rake	Thomas Armstrong	Head	38		Lead Ore Miner
	Mary Armstrong	Wife		34	
	Robert Armstrong	Son	17		Lead Ore Miner
	George Armstrong	Son	15		Lead Ore Washer
	Ann Armstrong	Daughter		13	
	Thomas Armstrong	Son	11		Lead Ore Washer
	John Spottswood	Son	6		
	Walton Spottswood	Son	3		
	Bartholomew Spottswood	Son	1		
	Ann Bell	Servant		15	House Servant
High Swinhope Mill	Joseph Philipson	Head	54		Farmer of 27 acres

Location	Name	Relation			Occupation
	Margaret Philipson	Wife		44	
	John Philipson	Son	9		
	Elizabeth Thirlwell	Servant		18	House Servant
High Swinhope Mill	John Whitfield	Head	33		Lead Ore Miner
	Ann Whitfield	Wife		30	
	Mary Whitfield	Daughter		7	
	Thomas Whitfield	Son	5		
	Hannah Whitfield	Daughter		3	
	John Whitfield	Son	1		
High Swinhope Mill	Ann Sparke	Head Widow		52	Miner's widow
	John Sparke	Son	26		Lead Ore Miner
	Mary Sparke	Daughter		19	
	Thomas Sparke	Son	12		
	Hannah Sparke	Daughter		10	
	James Sparke	Godson	4		
	John Sparke	Godson	1		
Swinhope Lodge	Isabella Sparke	Head Widow		76	Miner's widow
	Sarah Sparke	Daughter		35	
Swinhope Row	Mary Charlton	Head Widow		44	Shoe maker's widow
	Ann Charlton	Daughter		6	
Swinhope Row	Hannah Milburn	Head Widow		54	Miner's widow
	George Milburn	Son	20		Lead Ore Miner
	Thomas Milburn	Son	18		Lead Ore Miner
	John Charlton	Visitor	12		Scholar
	Hannah Elliott	Visitor		10	Scholar
Swinhope Row	Henry Milburn	Head	34		Lead Ore Miner
	Ann Milburn	Wife		24	
	Robert Milburn	Son	1		
Swinhope Mill	Elizabeth Whitfield	Head Widow		58	Grocer & Tea Dealer
	Elizabeth Whitfield	Daughter		20	
	George Whitfield	Son	19		Labourer
	John Whitfield	Son	17		Lead Ore Washer
	Teasdale Whitfield	Son	14		Lead Ore Washer
Swinhope Mill	George Coulson	Head	30		Lead Ore Miner
	? Coulson	Mother Widow		60	Miner's widow
Swinhope Mill	Joseph Ward	Head	28		Lead Ore Miner
	Jane Ward	Wife		23	
	Mary Ward	Daughter		3m	
Swinhope Mill	Elizabeth Dawson	Head Widow		32	Miner's widow
	Ann Dawson	Daughter		15	
	John Dawson	Son	11		Scholar

	Thomas Dawson	Son	8		
	Thompson Dawson	Son	6		Scholar
	William Dawson	Son	1		
	Anthony Charlton	Lodger	26		Lead Ore Miner
Swinhope Mill	John Dawson	Head	64		Lead Ore Washer
	Isabella Dawson	Wife		62	
	John Dawson	Son	33		Lead Ore Washer
	Abraham Dawson	Son	17		Lead Ore Washer
	Rebekah Armstrong	Servant		17	House Servant
Swinhope Mill	George Lee	Head	66		Retired Lead Ore Washer
	Jane Heslop	Servant		34	House Servant
Thorney Knowe	William Wilson	Head	35		Lead Ore Miner
	Hannah Wilson	Wife		37	
	John Parker	Son	8		Scholar
	Hannah Parker	Daughter		6	
	Mary Ann Parker	Daughter		3	
	Hannah Coulson	Servant		20	House Servant
Thorney Knowe	Joseph Kearton	Head	35		Labourer
	Ann Kearton	Wife		38	
	William Kearton	Son	9		
	Mary Kearton	Daughter		6	
	Joseph Kearton	Son	3		
	Ann Kearton	Daughter		6m	
Thorney Knowe	John Philipson	Head	49		Farmer of 30 acres
	Mary Philipson	Wife		43	
	John Philipson	Son	20		Labourer
	Ann Philipson	Daughter		17	
	George Philipson	Son	15		Scholar
	Mary Philipson	Daughter		12	
	Hannah Philipson	Daughter		10	Scholar
	Thompson Philipson	Son	7		
Elpha Green	George Milburn	Head	29		Lead Ore Miner
	Jane Milburn	Wife		27	
	Mary Milburn	Daughter		4	
Elpha Green	Mark Noble	Head	56		Lead Ore Miner
	Mary Noble	Wife		53	
	Ann Noble	Daughter		27	
	Mark Noble	Son	24		Lead Ore Miner
	Joseph Noble	Son	22		
	John Noble	Son	20		
	William Noble	Son	18		Pupil Teacher
	Sparke Noble	Son	16		Lead Ore Washer
	Lowes Noble	Son	14		Scholar
	Mary Noble	Daughter		12	Scholar

Place	Name	Relation	Age (M)	Age (F)	Occupation
	Hannah Noble	Daughter		9	Scholar
Elpha Green	Thomas Nattrass	Head	56		Retired Miner
	Ann Nattrass	Mother		89	Miner's widow
	Frances Nattrass	Sister		47	
Elpha Green	William Ward	Head	20		Lead Ore Miner
	Sarah Ward	Sister		25	
Swinhope Shield	John Curry	Head	62		Lead Ore Miner
	Elizabeth Curry	Sister		48	
	George Curry	Nephew	19		Lead Ore Miner
	Joseph Curry	Nephew	11		Scholar
	Hannah Johnson	Servant		16	House Servant
High Town	John Maughan	Head	29		Lead Ore Miner
	Mary Maughan	Wife		31	
	Mary Maughan	Daughter		5	
	John Maughan	Son	3		
	Hannah Maughan	Daughter		9m	
Swinhope Shield	Jonathon Shield	Head	55		Farmer of 60 acres
	Sarah Shield	Wife		45	
	Jane Shield	Daughter		21	
	Hugh Shield	Son	18		Labourer
	Jonathon Shield	Son	7		
	Sarah Shield	Daughter		1	
	Jane Shield	Visitor		47	
Swinhope Shield	James Waggott	Head	58		Lead Ore Miner
	Ann Waggott	Wife		53	
	Ann Waggott	Daughter		25	
	Elizabeth Waggott	Daughter		23	
	William Waggott	Son	21		Labourer
	Matthew Waggott	Son	16		Lead Ore Washer
Corn Mill	George Nevin	Head	53		Farmer & Miller
	Sarah Nevin	Wife		53	
	Margaret Nevin	Daughter		20	
	Mary Sparke	Servant		17	Servant
Corn Mill	Nevin Philipson	Head	39		Cartman
	Margaret Philipson	Wife		36	
	Thomas Philipson	Son	17		Lead Ore Washer
	Elizabeth Philipson	Daughter		13	
	John Philipson	Son	5		Scholar
	James Ward	Lodger	1		
Old Dyke	John Hunter	Head Widow	43		Retired Miner
	Bownass				
	Joseph Bownass	Son	17		Lead Ore Miner
	Maisy Bownass	Daughter		14	
	John Hunter	Son	12		Scholar

Bownass

Coating Hill	Nevin Reed	Head	43		Lead Ore Miner
	Phillis Reed	Wife		38	
	Mary Reed	Daughter		13	
	Hannah Reed	Daughter		11	
	Paul Reed	Son	9		Scholar
	Isaac Reed	Son	7		Scholar
	Ann Reed	Daughter		5	
	John Reed	Son	3		
	Nevin Reed	Son	8m		
Coating Hill	Joseph Graham	Head	37		Lead Ore Miner
	Mary Graham	Wife		31	
	Joseph Graham	Son	8		Scholar
	Elizabeth Graham	Daughter		7	
	Arthur Graham	Son	5		
	Jane Ann Graham	Daughter		4	
	Mary Graham	Daughter		2	
	John Graham	Son	3m		
Coating Hill	John Smith	Head	42		Quarryman
	Phillis Smith	Wife		37	
	William Smith	Son	18		Quarryman
	John Smith	Son	16		Quarryman
	Margaret Smith	Daughter		14	
	Hannah Smith	Daughter		12	Scholar
	Martha Smith	Daughter		10	Scholar
	Henry Smith	Son	8		Scholar
	Thomas Smith	Son	6		
	Esau Smith	Son	2		
	Mary Smith	Daughter		4m	
Hunt Well	Sarah Philipson	Head Widow		60	Miner's widow
	William Philipson	Son	23		Lead Ore Miner
	Edward Philipson	Son	21		Lead & Silver Smelter
	John Philipson	Son	16		Cartman
	Sarah Philipson	Daughter		15	House Servant
Hunt Well	Jane Milburn	Head Widow		56	Miner's widow
	Jane Milburn	Daughter		27	
	Cowin Milburn	Son	25		Lead Ore Miner
	Isabella Milburn	Daughter		23	
	Mary Milburn	Daughter		19	
	Thomas Milburn	Son	17		Cartman
	John Milburn	Son	15		Lead Ore Miner
	Matthew Milburn	Son	13		
Hunt Well	Joseph Graham	Head	60		Retired Miner
	Elizabeth Graham	Wife		62	
	Mary Graham	Daughter		33	Bonnet maker
	Thomas Graham	Son	31		Lead Ore Miner

	Ann Graham	Daughter		28	Bonnet maker
	Abraham Graham	Son	26		Lead Ore Miner
	Elizabeth Graham	Daughter		23	
	Gilbert Graham	Son	21		Cartman
	Jane Graham	Daughter		19	
	Margaret Graham	Daughter		16	
Hunt Well	James Pearson	Head	47		Lead Ore Miner
	William Pearson	Brother	55		Lead Ore Miner
	Hannah Pearson	Wife		36	
	Mary Pearson	Daughter		12	
	John Pearson	Son	11		Scholar
	Joseph Pearson	Son	8		Scholar
	Ann Pearson	Daughter		6	Scholar
	William Pearson	Son	3		
	James Pearson	Son	1		
	Thomas Armstrong	Servant	24		Labourer
Black Lotment	Henry Philipson	Head	51		Lead Ore Miner
	Sarah Philipson	Wife		44	
	Sarah Philipson	Daughter		20	Dressmaker
	Nicholas Philipson	Son	16		Lead Ore Washer
	John Philipson	Son	13		Lead Ore Washer
	Ann Philipson	Daughter		10	
	Elizabeth Philipson	Daughter		7	
	Henry Philipson	Son	4		
	Margaret Philipson	Daughter		4m	

Allendale Estate Rents - 1847

OWNER	ADDRESS	ACRES	RENT
Thomas Wentworth Beaumont	Swinhope Mill	35	
"	Nether Coatenhill	34	
"	Upper Coatenhill	32	
"	Old Dyke	17	
"	Side House	14	
"	Peasmeadows	25	
"	Corn Mill	3	
"	Scots Meadows	29 + 52	
George Coulson	Swinhope Mill	3	3 shillings
Hannah Milburn	Swinhope Mill	2	2 "
John Philipson	Elpha Green	15	15 "
John Philipson	Swinhope Shield	6	6 "
Matthew & Isaac Lee	Shield Bank	57	£3
Thomas Stephenson	Middlehope	44	50 shillings
Joseph Philipson	Swinhope Shield	14	30 "
	& Black Cleugh	19	
Thos & Jacob Mathas	Black Cleugh	6	6 "
William Crawhall	Hammershield		£18 + others
John Lee	Middlehope	20	£1
Heirs of John Hull	Intake Head	24	24 shillings
Jonathon Shield	Swinhope Shield	47	50 "
Henry Philipson	Sparty Lea - 1/3	17	£1
George Philipson	Sparty Lea - 2/3		
John Dixon	Sipton Shield	24	6 shillings
Joseph & Christopher Pears	Middlehope	26	6 "
George Robson	Elpha Green	39	9 "
	& Shield Close		
Joseph Currey	Ellershope	46	9 "
John Coulson	Swinhope Mill	10	3 "
Joseph Philipson	Elpha Green	15	6 "
Thomas Sparke	Round Hill	20	3 "
John Philipson &			
Ann Noble	Elpha Green	31	6 "
Isabella Lee	Shield Bank	28	6 "

Property Rents & Rateable Values 1876

OCCUPIER	OWNER	PROPERTY	GROSS ESTIMATED RENTAL	RATEABLE VALUE
John Liddle	W B Beaumont	Swinhope Shield House & Land	£29	£27
Joseph Whitfield	"	"	£15-10-0	£14-5-0
John Liddle	"	House only	£4-10-0	£4
Abraham Dawson	"	Swinhope Mill House & Land	£21	£19-10-0
Matthew Lee	"	"	£21	£10-10-0
Thomas Bell	"	Swinhope Head	£3	£2-10-0
John Hewitson	"	Meadow Cottage	£8	£8-10-0
Sarah Roddam	"	Scotch Meadows House & Land	£12	£11
John Philipson	"	"	£18	£16-15-0
Christopher Roddam	"	"	£16-5-0	£14-15-0
Thomas Whitfield	"	Scotch Meadows	£12-15-0	£11-15-0
Elizabeth McMillan	"	Shaw House	£21	£19-10-0
Robert McMillan	"	"	£22	£20-10-0
John Coats	"	Hammershields	£67-10-0	£62-10-0
Hannah Robson	"	Middlehope Green	£27-10-0	£25-10-0
Jane Milburn	"	Huntwell	£33-5-0	£30-15-0
Cowing Milburn	"	"	£35	£32-10-0
Gilbert Graham	"	"	£38	£35-5-0
George Robson	"	"	£17	£15-15-0
Mrs Smith	"	Upper Cotenhill	£16	£14-15-0
John Milburn	"	Cotenhill	£14	£13
Phillis Reed	"	Nether Cotenhill	£18	£16-10-0
William Charlton	"	Cotenhill	£13	£12-5-0
Henry Robson	"	Old Dyke	£7-10-0	£7
W Beaumont	"	Corn Mill, Tilery & House	£10	£9
W Sparke	"	Corn Mill, House & Land & Mill	£120	£108

Name	Owner	Property	Value	Value
George Vickers	"	Ellershope Shield	£14	£13
Henry Philipson	"	Side House	£17	£15-15-0
Dr Davis	"	Elia House	£21	£19-10-0
William Hutchinson	"	Breckon Hill	£7	£6-10-0
Nicholas Lee	"	Breckon Holm	£16	£14-15-0
Ann Heslop	"	Peasmeadows House	£4	£3-10-0
Joseph Reed	"	House x 3	£3-15-0	£3-5-0
Mary Dargue	"	House	£4	£3-10-0
Jane Curry	"	House x 2	£4	£3-10-0
Matthew Ridley	"	House	£4	£3-10-0
Hannah Bright	"	House x 2 & Land	£11	£10-15-0
Elizabeth Milburn	"	House & Land	£9-5-0	£8-10-0
William Walton	"		£31-10-0	£29-5-0
Francis Hewitson		Byrehope		
Ann Dargue		House & Land	£8	£7-10-0
Mark Hewitson	"	"	£8-10-0	£8
Ann Hewitson	"	"	£8	£7-10-0
Anthony Johnson	"	"	£7-10-0	£7
Thomas Short	"	"	£8	£7-10-0
Sarah Hewitson	"	"	£8-10-0	£8
Thomas Heslop	"	"	£9	£8-5-0
Andrew Liddle	"	"	£8-10-0	£8
John Philipson	"	"	£7-10-0	£7
Isaac Reed	Lord Allendale	Tileworks Cottage	£15	£14
Isaac Reed	John Watson	Swinhope Shield	£32-15-0	£30-5-0
Ann Waggot	John Watson	"	£25-5-0	£23-10-0
Thomas Forster	William Oliver	"	£43-5-0	£40
John Parker	John Glenwright	Elpha Green	£20	£18
George Philipson	Mark Noble		£18	£16-15-0
Matthew Reed	George Philipson	Swinhope Mill	£10-10-0	£7-15-0
"	Thomas Coulson	Thorney Knowe	£2-5-0	£2
"	"	Land	£12	£11
John Pigg	Heirs of John Philipson	Allotment House	£10-10-0	£9-15-0
Jane Milburn	Robert Coulson	"	£3-10-0	£3
Robert Coulson	"	Land	£10	£9-5-0

Occupier	Owner	Property		
Paul Wilkinson	J Simpson	Low Hayrake	£28	£26
Robert Milburn	"	House & Land	£20	£10-10-0
Robson Reed	"	High Hayrake	£12	£11
	"	Black Cleugh	£25-10-0	£23-15-0
		House & Land	£12	£11
John Hull	Mary Nattrass	Intack	£4	£3-10-0
John Reed	Robson Reed	Black Cleugh	£3-10-0	£3
Robson Reed	Richard Medcalf	Pry House	£11	£10-5-0
William Reed		"	£3-10-0	£3
James Reed	Messers Reed	Pry House & Land	£1-10-0	£1-10-0
		Hope Head	£2-10-0	£2-5-0
		"	£15-17-0	£14-15-0
		"	£16-17-0	£15-0-0
Walton Reed	J Mulcaster	House & Land	£17	£15-15-0
John Reed	"	"	£17	£15-15-0
Thomas McMillan	"	Moss House	£12	£11
Matthew Varty	Mssrs Grevick & Renwick	House & Land	£25	£23-5-0
Richard Noble	"	"	£19	£17-10-0
Harrison McMillan	"	Stripe House	£29	£27
Thomas Renwick	Rev Thos Jones	Hayrake	£4	£3-10-0
John Philipson	Ann Bell	White Ridge	£4	£3-10-0
Hannah Pearson	Matthew Varty	Green Pitts	£4	£3-10-0
George Craven	John Varty	"	£8	£7-10-0
John Varty	Matthew Varty	"	£10-10-0	£9-15-0
Richard Medcalf	Thomas Varty	"	£15-10-0	£14-10-0
Thomas Varty	Joseph Varty	"	£4	£3-10-0
Elizabeth Varty	Elizabeth McMillan	Guide Post		
Ruth Pearson	George Pears	Middlehope	£7	£6-10-0
John Walton		House & Land	£14	£13
Matthew Robson	John Ashman	"		

Half Yearly House Rents for 1905

		£	s	d
St Peter's School Water Rate			5	0
Thos Bell (Rept)	Meadow Cottage	5	12	6
Archibold Bright	Intake	4	5	6
John Bright (Rept)	Sipton	9	15	0
W Bright	Sipton	5	12	6
Stephen Charlton	Byrehope	6	0	0
Ann Dargue (Rept)	Byrehope	4	5	6
John Dargue	Byrehope	5	0	0
Gilbert Graham (Rept)	Huntwell	16	15	0
Harrison J Heslop	Byrehope	5	18	6
Harrison J Heslop	Byrehope	4	16	6
Mary & Jacob Hull	Swinhope	7	18	2
Nicholas Lee	Breckon Holme	9	0	0
Nicholas Lee	Side House & Round Hill	16	10	0
Nicholas Liddle	Byrehope	20	6	6
Nicholas Liddle	Peasmeadows Garden		2	6
Christopher Liddle	Sparty Lea	10	16	3
William Liddle	Swinhope Shield	23	5	6
Thompson Lee	Swinhope	12	0	0
Joseph McMillan	Shaw House	9	7	6
Joseph Midcalf	Swinhope Edge	4	14	4
Jane Milburn (Rept)	Huntwell	15	7	6
John Milburn (Rept)	Coatinghill	5	14	6
Elizabeth & William MacMillan	Caple Shaw	9	7	6
Thos MacMillan	Scotch Meadows	18	0	0
Wm Nixon (Rept) & Robson	Hammershields	35	10	0
Harrison Nixon	Peasmeadows Garden		2	6
Hannah & Joseph Noble	Cornmill	37	10	0
John Philipson (Rept)	Scotch Meadows	22	3	1
John Parker	Burnfoot	18	15	0
George Philipson	Coatinghill	6	1	0
John Philipson	Tedham	6	11	3
Matthew Philipson	Sipton	1	10	0
John Pigg	Tedham	7	17	6
George Robson	Huntwell	7	10	6
Jos Robson (Rept)	Shield Bank	16	0	0
Nevin Reed	Coatinghill	8	1	0
William Renwick	Huntwell	15	13	6

William Robson	Old Dyke	5 - 3 - 6
Joseph Reed	Swinhope Mill	10 - 0 - 0
Walton Reed	Tilery Cottage	1 - 10
John Reed	Hope Head	14 - 0 - 9
John Smith (Rept)	Coatinghill	6 - 10 - 6
John Smith (Rept)	Byrehope Bank	5 - 0
W H Sparke	Peasmeadows	10 - 10 - 0
W H Sparke & others	Elia	8 - 0 - 0
Wm Sparke (Rept)	Intake	4 - 3 - 6
John Sparke (Rept)	Middlehope Green	10 - 10 - 0
Thos Sparke (Rept)	Elia	5 - 5 - 0
Ralph Sparke	Elia	5 - 5 - 0
Joseph Sparke (Rept)	Sparty Lea	6 - 5 - 6
Vicar of St Peter's Water Leave		
Joseph Vickers	Meadow Cottage	3 - 5 - 0
Ann Woodmas	Sipton	1 - 10 - 0
Post Master General	Telegraph Poles	5 - 0 yearly
		due 1 August

These rents were paid to the Allendale Estates.

Various Rentals

ALLENHEADS TOLL RENTS:
1904 - Jan - May   8 shillings
  "   - May - Dec   5 shillings
1905 - May - Dec   5-6d
VIEILLE MONTAGNE & CO COALCLEUGH:
1903 - 05   Rents from: Farms & Cottages - £175-0-0 per half year   due May & Nov
                          Mines - £175-0-0 per half year   due Jan & July
                          Crow Coal - £15-0-0 per half year   due Jan & July
COALCLEUGH SHOOTING MOORS:
1903 - 05   £120-0-0 per year
STUBBLICK SHOOTING MOOR:
1903 - 05   Walter Scott £510 per year. Lease extended 3 years from 1 Jan 1906
ALLENDALE ESTATES ABSTRACT OF RENTAL:
Year ending Dec 1905:

	Arrears	Amount collected
Allenheads	£147-10-10	£ 866-1-10
		£1108-11-10
Allen Mill	£ 28-17-9	£ 653-4-4
		£1425-16-0
Coalcleugh	5-0d	£ 677-10-0

Jack Reed of Shield Close and George Stobbs, carter, from Allendale

Making hay at High Shield c. 1900. Bob Sparke of Allendale (seated)
and Jack Reed of Shield Close

A Lovely Day

There's nothing better to lighten the spirit
Than a stroll over Whetstone Mea,
As the curlew, plover and lapwing,
And wild flowers
Wake up to the day.

Killhope Law towering above you,
While the bent and heather sway.
The 'Heads and Swinhope below you,
Smoking chimneys
To welcome the day.

Tales of the miners and farmers
Haunting the green road's way,
As you wander towards the Hope Head –
A lonely bastle
At the heart of the day.

A view from the old Swinhope Chapel:
There's Lloyd at White Hills making hay;
Susie's sun lounge, and St Peter's school bell
Silent now
In the peace of the day.

It's a country patchwork before you,
Stone dykes round green fields, lambs at play.
There's the bus away up the valley and
Elsom's trailer
Back from Hexham Mart Day.

Then it's down through Old Dyke to the Corn Mill.
At Sparty Lea the ponies will neigh.
Greet the chaps tending the churchyard
For the folks
From a bygone day.

Between Hammershield and Peasmeadows
The kestrel hovers – as it sights its prey.
And it's home by the bridge and High Huntwell,
The end
Of a lovely day.

Jennifer Norderhaug
1986

Bastle Houses

Bastle houses and pele towers are a typical feature of the Northumbrian and Border landscapes. They represent the lawless, tough and insecure nature of our history.

In the 14th and 15th centuries the Borders were rife with feuding and looting, murder and theft. Outrageous acts were perpetrated between the English and the Scots but also between rival families on the same side of the Border. No-one was safe. Loyalty was almost non-existent in that one week the Armstrongs may link with the Ridleys to raid the Charltons, then the next week the Armstrongs may join forces with the Charltons to steal back their property from the Ridleys. Livestock was the prime target and cattle and sheep and horses had to be kept under lock and key.

Such was the situation in the time of the Border Reivers. In order to attempt some form of control the whole region of Northern England and Southern Scotland from east to west coasts was divided into Marches and a Warden was put in charge of each March to enforce law and order. It was an unenviable task.

Sparty Lea would fall into the English Middle March. The wealthier folk built for their protection a type of tower called a pele where they could have their cattle on the ground floor and live themselves on the first floor. Some of these peles still remain, the best one locally being the Vicar's Pele in Corbridge Market Place which can be viewed and gives a splendid idea of the existence people were forced to endure sometimes for weeks on end when a raid was in operation.

Local surnames evident today are true Border Reiver family names, e.g. Armstrong, Ridley, Charlton, Carr or Kerr, Beattie, Bell, Burn, Dodd, Elliott, Forster, Graham, Scott, Rutherford, Robson, Nixon, Hall, Little, Milburn, Johnstone. Many of these names occur in the annals of Sparty Lea history.

Bastles were built, on order of the King, as protection mainly by ordinary farmers as their everyday home - a sad reflection on the times that such measures needed to be taken as a matter of course. Fortified farmhouses, or bastles, appeared throughout the Border region between 1575 and 1650. The ground floor was equipped for the cattle and the first floor for the family so that a man and all his possessions could be securely locked up for the night when most raids took place under cover of darkness.

The majority of bastles appear to have been generally of a standard size - a rectangular structure 9m x 6m with walls up to 1.2m thick built of rubble and stones with huge corner stones and door and window lintels. There would be a single doorway into the ground level byre and a trapdoor in the ceiling would give access to the living accommodation above which would be heated by an open fire with central heating created by a byre full of warm cattle "below stairs"!

A wooden removable ladder would give access to the first floor through an external door often in the south wall. Later bastles which survived and were used as homes in more peaceful times had a stone stairway constructed up to the first floor door. Windows would be barred by heavy iron grills and the door was of stout wood with an inner drawbar to slide into a slot in the thick walls.

Door lintels would usually be of one single immense stone with a semicircular or flat pointed arch in the Allendale area. Two such bastles remain in the Swinhope valley - at Hope Head and Low Hayrake. The latter has been altered almost out of recognition although it is possible to detect some of the original features but Hope Head, although now attached to a much later building, is an outstanding example and thought to be one of the oldest houses in the area. Shorngate stood near the Durham county boundary above Allenheads, the highest house in England and possibly the oldest.

Low Hayrake, Swinhope

Low Hayrake is situated further down the Swinhope valley and just off the green track leading from Carrshield to Sparty Lea. The building has been extensively modernised and very little of the former bastle as it would have been is now visible.

It is known, however, that Low Hayrake is an extended bastle, i.e. where a second slightly larger bastle has been built on to the gable end of the first bastle, the later building still being a true bastle with ground floor byre etc.

The north gable shows a first floor doorway. Downstairs rooms are 2m40cm high, external walls 1m thick. Upstairs window ledges are 80cm thick with very old beams in evidence and the chimney breast is 71cm deep and 3m30cm in height.

Above: Dickson Nicholl, Sparty Lea postman and farmer, riding along the track to Hope Head to deliver mail.

Below & Right: Hope Head with bastle doorway 1987; the house is currently being renovated.

Hope Head, Swinhope

Situated at the head of the Swinhope valley, Hope Head is the last house and one of the few remaining good examples of a bastle.

Measuring 9.6m x 6.5m it is now joined to a building thought to have been added in the 18th century. The bastle faces ESE and lies at the head of the Swinhope valley on a green track which used to run from Carrshield to Sparty Lea. From Hope Head the track is very easy to follow to Sparty Lea, the stretch over the moor westward has become overgrown.

Below the bastle can be seen the disused Swinhope Lead Mine and the now empty and grassed over Swinhope Reservoir. The adjoining cottage is a holiday home but was permanently inhabited and the land farmed until quite recently. The building is without electricity. Notable features are the byre door in the north end, the first floor door and windows which are visible internally. There is an 18th century fireplace with evidence of an earlier hood.

In the rear wall is a first floor door and below the door is a small window 40 centimetres from the ground measuring 53cm high and 43cm wide. Another window is 2.30m from the ground with a heavy stone lintel and measures 48cm high and 43cm wide.

The most interesting feature lies in the NNE facing gable end wall - a doorway leading to a stone flagged room. There are huge sockets on the inside of the door jambs and a heavy stone lintel across the top of the entrance on the inside measuring 40cm wide and 79cm long.

The door stands 1.60m high from the ground, is 79cm wide and the external wall at the doorway is 1.23m thick. Three rounded corner stones form the entrance, the largest being 71cm high and 20cm wide. The lintel over the door is in the shape of a pointed arch. A line of stone slabs form a pathway leading from the door to the front of the bastle.

The surrounding flora is typical upland - bents or sparts, heather, bracken, wild orchids and the birdlife includes a short-eared owl, curlew, lapwing, grouse and golden plover. Ring ouzel have also been heard here.

Hope Head has now been sold and is being renovated and inhabited by a family making it once again into a home.

Shorngate, Allenheads

Sited to the west of the Allenheads-Rookhope road above East End Reservoir was another bastle, Shorngate. Louis Robson's family lived there at one time. The earthwork named the Black or Scotch Dyke enters the county by the property before running up the valley towards Catton Old Town. Until recently Shorngate was reduced to a pile of stones. Today those stones have been reused to build Shorngate House in Hexham.

The following article appeared in the Northern Echo on Saturday, October 10 1932:

John Roddam at Shorngate 1932

Northumberland's Oldest and Highest House

BY A NORTHERN ECHO REPORTER

I had the privilege yesterday of paying a visit to the oldest house in Northumberland.

It occupies an imposing site upon the top of a hill overlooking Allenheads, about two miles across the border line of Durham and Northumberland.

The little house or cottage which is known as Shaungate, is in a wonderful state of preservation and it bears evidence that many buildings in that part of Northumberland were built by the Romans.

Mr. and Mrs. J. Roddam and their family of three young children occupy the house and they are proud of it. They enjoy the freedom of an open-air life and consequently every member of the household is in a splendid state of health.

Not only is their house the oldest in Northumberland but it is the highest. It is perched upon a lofty ridge 2,000 feet above sea level, and visitors standing in the cobble-stoned yard command a view of the heather-clad moors and the Pennine Range.

Shorngate   1932

The new Shorngate House being built with stone from the original.

The blacksmith's shop, Allenheads c.1910

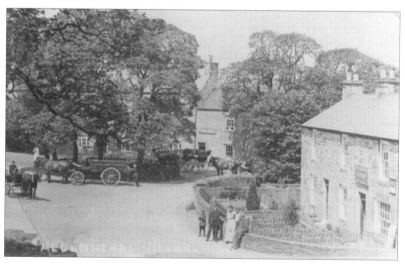

Allenheads village, c.1900, with the Allenheads Inn and the bullring
where cattle and horses were tethered.

Lead Mining at Allenheads

Three miles up the valley from Sparty Lea lies Allenheads, England's highest village, between 404 and 442 metres.

Once the site of one of the largest lead mines producing one-seventh of England's lead in the late 18th and early 19th centuries, Allenheads is now better known as a prime location for grouse shooting. Allenheads Hall built in 1847 and one-time home for Thomas Sopwith has become a shooting lodge for Lord Allendale's estate.

Following the meandering River East Allen, the valley road snakes its way ever higher until it forks to provide two gateways to the village. The upper road leads past miners' cottages and the now capped Gin Hill Shaft towards The Hall and then forks passing Allenheads School building to Rookhope or Weardale, the end of the county.

The lower road descends to the river at the Smelt Mill Bridge where we find the old smelt mill and peat house. A side road aptly named Slag Hill passes two elliptical plan lime kilns to return to Sparty Lea or go further to Nenthead. From the smelt mill the lower road winds through terraces of miners' cottages at Ropehaugh and Dirtpot - names recalling the lead and smelt industries. Dirtpot was once renamed Dovespool.

The road passes the now closed Methodist Chapel, built in 1900 and closed in 2000. This building replaced a previous one built in 1834, then rebuilt in 1840 further along the road. It was a Wesleyan Methodist Chapel, the Primitive Methodist Church being in the old Youth Hostel which is now an Outdoor Centre. After passing the Church (1825), the horseshoe arched entrance to the Fawside Level (1776) and the Allenheads Lead Mine yard, the lower road eventually reaches the 18th century Allenheads Inn at the tiny square where once also stood a petrol station and post office.

In 1689 the Allenheads mines were purchased by Sir William Blackett of Newcastle. His estate, due to there being no male heir, passed to the Beaumont family and Sir Wentworth Blackett became the first Lord Allendale.

In the 17th, 18th and 19th centuries lead mining was big business in the dales. Three main companies controlled production - the Weardale Lead Co., the London Lead Co., and the Blackett-Beaumont Lead Co., the latter owning the Allendale mines.

In the heydays about one-seventh of the total lead produced in the country came from this area with an exceptionally high silver content. In 1842 the Blackett-

Beaumont Company employed more than 2,000 people in Allendale and Weardale, i.e. two-fifths of the total number of miners.

In 1869 Allen and Weardale mines produced 10,402 tons of lead ore yielding 9,407 tons of lead and 52,486 ounces of silver. Tynehead mines, near Source of Tyne walk, produced silver for the Royal Mint in Carlisle and those miners had preferential treatment. In 1851 a silver cake was entered from the Allendale mines into the Great Exhibition in London weighing 12,162 ounces and valued at £3,344.

The Blackett-Beaumont Company was a "family" firm in that the Company cared for the social as well as economic side of the miner and his family's lives. Chapels were built, schools provided and small acreages let with cottages for the keeping of a few sheep, pigs, cows, etc. Before young boys were given mine employment they had to complete a certain amount of schooling to read and write. In the 1823 Company Bargain Book only a handful of men needed to sign their names with a cross. By 1842 gross exploitation of the young had ceased and 10 was the minimum age for boys to enter the washing floors. A 10-year-old would earn 7d per day.

Miners were employed on a Bargain System and usually six or seven men would team together as Partners and would strike a Bargain with the Company to be paid for bringing so many bings (1 bing = 8cwt) of lead ore to the surface or for digging so many fathoms to create or maintain levels. Often there would be up to five levels in one mine including the horse level which was always stone arched. The first Bargain was struck in 1751 when Thomas Bell agreed to drive 10 fathoms at 20s per fathom and to receive 20s for all the ore he mined.

Payment was made twice yearly with a subsistence allowance (lent money) paid in between. This "sub" plus charges for candles, washers, gunpowder, etc. were deducted from the miner's pay and, if he had had a bad spell, he could frequently end up owing the Company money on Pays Day which was also a festival day in the villages.

Between March and June 1793 the pay bill for the Company was £2,944 paid to 275 miners - an average of £10.14s per man for 13 weeks' work. The schoolmaster was paid £2.10s for the term and the blacksmiths 10s6d per week. Including ancilliary workers the total pay bill for the period was £3,904. In that time 756 tons of lead ore had been raised, 697 tons going to the Dukesfield Smelt Mill. The market price of pig lead that year was £19 per ton.

Conditions in lead mines were poor with much water and bad air but there were fewer fatalities in lead mines than in coal mines. Many miners walked miles to work on a Monday morning and lodged all week in a Mine Shop. There were more deaths from contagious illnesses passed in the Mine Shop, with 10 or 12 men sleeping head to toe, than in the mines.

The lead ore was transported on galloway ponies to the smelt mills at Dukesfield, Langley and Allendale via Carrier tracks still wending their now empty ways over the moors today. From the smelt mills the lead went to the east coast ports. Smelting was a separate skilled trade and rarely did a smelter work in a mine.

Smelting was a highly skilled job and smelters rarely mixed with miners. The basic principle of smelting was to reduce the ore to pure lead by heating in a blast of air. Oxygen in the air oxidised the sulphur so leaving behind lead. All smelt mills were sited near water which provided the power for the bellows. Fuel for the furnaces was taken in the form of peat or wood.

The ore, or galena, from each vein was stored separately in the smelt mill and ore from the same vein was sent periodically to different mines to test the skill and care of individual smelters.

A system of industrial training was in operation at each mill. Boys started out on the washing floor with miners' sons but the 1851 census shows that smelters' sons always followed their fathers into smelting. A young man would begin as a labourer before becoming the second in a two man team. If good enough he would progress to the highest rank of refiner. The London Lead Company even sent their chief smelters on chemistry courses to Durham University. There was much competition and piracy between mills with smelters often moving from one mill to another. This rarely happened with miners.

Smelters usually occupied the best houses and they were paid according to the weight of lead or number of pigs produced – the Blackett/Beaumonts paying by the ton. In 1809 Dukesfield Mill smelters were paid 9s 8d per week as there were more men whereas, with fewer men at the Allen Mill in Allendale, smelters received 14s 6d per week. Normal shifts lasted 12-15 hours as the furnaces, once hot, had to be kept burning.

The fumes created by the smelting process were highly toxic and eventually flues were built to take the fumes away from the mills to isolated spots on the moors, each flue ending in a tall chimney.

Entrance to the Blackett Level, below Allendale Town.

A train of galloway ponies crossing the moors carrying lead for smelting.

The Allendale flues were constructed in the early 1800s, the first one originally ending at Cleugh Head, near Thornley Gate, but later extended to join the second flue. Together these flues measure about five miles and they were periodically cleaned by boys to salvage the lead deposits and also the silver. It was estimated that the sweeping of these flues annually harvested silver worth £6,000-10,000.

Smelting was a seasonal job as winter passage over the lead routes made transportation impossible and fuel stocks of peat would be frozen. Smelters were then employed on drainage, hedging, etc.

Transport of lead to Newcastle was a major problem for the Company and in the 18th century they paid out more on transport than on smelting. By 1830 the Newcastle-Carlisle Railway had solved the problem but trains of galloways were still used as late as 1880.

The arrival of Thomas Sopwith, as Chief Agent to the Beaumont family from 1845-71, brought much improvement in conditions both in the mines and for the families. His friendship with Lord Armstrong of Cragside gave him access to some of the most up-to-date hydraulic technology of the day. The water was extracted from the mines and a complex system of reservoirs and water races set up to use and re-use the water for various purposes.

His greatest undertaking was the construction of the Blackett Level - a tunnel to be driven over six miles from Allendale to Allenheads. Its object was to draw water from the mines and to find new lead veins. The level had four shafts, the deepest of 71 fathoms, but sadly it only reached 4¾ miles to Sparty Lea by the time the price of lead was beginning to fall. Only a small amount of lead was ever brought from the Blackett Level but it cost Mr Beaumont upwards of £250,000.

Lead mining virtually ceased up here about 1910. Although still much lead was left, it was no longer viable to mine with prices so much cheaper from elsewhere. At its peak in 1805 the market price of lead was £35 per bing, by 1885 that had slumped to £12. In the late 1890s, with the writing on the wall, many dales lead miners emigrated to America.

Walter White visits Allenheads

The following extracts come from an account of a visit to Allenheads made by Walter White. They appear in his work "Northumberland and the Border" 1859:

We pass St Peter's, the mother church of the dale, then the little village of Dirtpot - what a name! - lying in the hollow; then we come to rows of workshops, long rows of bouseteams and bingsteads on each side of an acre or more of washing floors, where men and boys are working with noise and activity, a wooden tower within which is one of the entrances of the lead mines; a row of buildings containing the offices, the library and reading room, and we are in Allenheads, one of the most elevated places in England, situated 1400 feet above the sea.

The people about here are all employed in mining operations and I am told that Allenheads is to be regarded as the nucleus, containing a few shops and an inn, of the houses scattered over this part of the dale rather than as a village. On a level above the rest stands a large house, one of Mr Beaumont's residences with a pleasant garden and shrubberies about it. In a commanding position on the opposite side of the valley stands the schoolhouse enjoying or not, according to the weather, a wide prospect. Below it, approached by a tree-bordered causeway is the chapel of ease.

It was significant at the locality that the carriage could not draw up to the gate of this house, because of two deep holes that had sunk a few days before, by the giving way of something underground. They had, it is true, been filled up more than once with refuse from the washing floor, but who could tell whether they might not sink again with the weight of a carriage? So it was best to be cautious. It may be exciting, but certainly is not comfortable to live in a place where the bottom of your cellar may fall out without warning, or you may step from your door into a pit which has opened in the night. However, if miners will dig out the heart of the hills they must take the consequences.

Not only the hilltops, but the whole landscape was white with snow the next morning; the washing floor could not begin work in consequence till near noon. I could not help thinking that Allenheads must be the place where a stranger afflicted by the terrible weather asked "Does it always rain here?" and got for answer "Na, it snaws whiles". But when a fine day does occur it is worth ten of the fine days that gladden the lowlands. In some years the quantity of rain is double that which falls in Middlesex and it is a good year which has a hundred days free from rain or snow. The inhabitants are lucky in having employment underground out of the way of foul weather.

Mr Beaumont, aided by the subscriptions of other gentlemen, has built new schoolhouses in different parts of the district. The old makeshift has been replaced by new washing floors, new offices, new storehouses and workshops, and proper machinery. Mr Beaumont aids the Benefit Society Fund by an annual contribution of five per cent of the year's subscriptions and of two per cent on all properly invested funds. Lectures to the miners and books for prizes to the school are occasionally given by Mr Sopwith.

So good a schoolhouse as that which stands high up on the slope, with a wide outlook over hill and valley, deserved a good schoolmaster, and a good one it has - a Scotsman. The boys' school is at one end of the building, the girls at the other; the residence of the Master and Mistress between the two. I was in the school a minute before nine, yet every scholar was in place, though some had come two or three miles; and punctuality is the rule. The place was built ten years ago, but the plaster is sound and unblemished and the forms and desks are as clean and unblemished as new. You look in vain for an inkstain, or for the notching and hacking usual where the boys carry pocket knives, as these do. Mr Sopwith thought that a habit of punctuality, of order and cleanliness, of the self-restraint induced by the avoidance of mischief would not only have a beneficial effect on the children, present and prospective, but through them on the parents; and he was not mistaken.

What a clattering there was of brass-clasped clogs on the stone floor as the girls came into the boys' school to take part in the singing and prayer with which the daily duty commences. Then followed more singing during which, at my request, they had leave to sing anything they liked best, and it was a pleasure to hear with what spirit they struck up "will you, will you, will you, will you come to the woods!" and with the more effect from their having a pretty fair notion of harmony, while the Master joined in with his musical bass. Then when it was time for the girls to retire, the boys with a one-two-three-four marching tune sang them out.

The classes showed me how expert they were in arithmetic, how well they could write, and books full of drawings in which the progress from year to year was obvious. Many a man might envy these miners' children their skill with the pencil. Then followed an object lesson, and when he came to the egg the Master mentioned that in all the time he had charge of Allenheads school there was but one boy who pulled a bird's nest. And he told how that once when he asked the school if they knew what a mat was, a little fellow named Matthew stood forward and said, "Please Sir, I's a Mat".

"All you that have seen the sea hold up your hands", said the Master. Among 40 or 50 children, three raised their hands. They had once been to Tynemouth with their parents.

Allenheads Hall

Allenheads Hall was built on the site of a ruinous hamlet, named Craig House, in 1845, as a residence for Thomas Sopwith, chief agent of Mr Beaumont's lead mines. The architect was Mr E.B.Lamb whose brief was to spend no more than £4,000. In later years was used as a shooting lodge for Lord Allendale's family.

"Hold up your hands, all of you that have seen wheat growing." Five hands were held up.

At first it seems almost incredible that anyone in England had not seen wheat growing. It is, however, a fact that demonstrates the elevation of Allenheads above sea level. And if we remember that village children are not travellers, and that to see wheat growing the children here must go seven miles down to Allentown, we need not attribute the fewness of the hands held up, as some have, to a species of heathenism.

The miners' wages vary from 15 shillings to 20 shillings a week; payment is made by advance of two pounds "subsidence money" every four weeks and the balance once a year. In contrasting the amount with their labour, we must bear in mind that the miner's day is but eight hours and for five days only in the week. Hence they have much time to work for themselves, if they will, in their gardens or fields. Their great ambition is to possess a little freehold and many of them save money enough to accomplish their desire; and you may see their cottages scattered on the hillsides, showing cheerful patches of green around them. They have a Benefit Society and a Building Society, both flourishing. With respect to the former, it is worthy of remark that not one has yet applied for a deferred annuity payable at the age of 70. Not one expects to live to 70.

After two hours in the school, I went back to my room, put on a miner's suit of fustian, a rough round-crowned broad-brimmed hat, and then made myself over for a while to Mr Curry, inspector of the mine. It was almost like going down a well to descend the shaft, so copious is the drip from the sides. The depth is 77 fathoms, but we stopped at a level - or random as the miners call it - 42 fathoms down, and there getting into a narrow wagon, each holding a candle stuck into a lump of clay, were driven away at a trot, "to the west end of Henry". If you feel crushed in a coal mine then much more so here where the ways are so narrow but little wider than the wagon, and you must sit still if you would avoid bruising your head against the limestone. Having rattled on a mile and a half, I learnt that Henry was the name of the vein; and here we got out and walked, and I saw how the vein of lead had been in places eight or nine feet thick, how it thinned off in places to an inch or two, in places to nothing, and was only traceable by the black line in the rock where the smooth shining surfaces come together, known to miners as slickensides. I saw veins of fluorspar, intersected by threads of metal, and the various strata - limestone, shales and clay - and in one of the veins a number of cavities full of beautiful crystals: wondrously beautiful they looked in the candlelight, like fairy grottos. We crawled at times on hands and knees; we climbed and descended perpendicular ladders 20 fathoms or more, through openings so narrow that with an inch or two additional breadth of shoulder you would stick. And so we came to the forehead or

Allenheads Lead Mine with the washing bays in the foreground c.1900

Workers at Allenheads Mine dressing floor c.1870.

one of the utmost extremities, where the men were working naked to the waist, and the heat and closeness were sickening.

When I saw the 40 horse hydraulic engines doing all the work of the mines - the winding, the pumping, the hotching, driving a newly invested slime separating machine - I felt the sight was worth the journey to Allendale. It seems to me there is a touch of real genius in thus demonstrating the importance and availability of natural power; a power that does duty quietly, requiring not to roar tremendously when it stops, as if to say, See how clever I am! There is no steam engine used at any of Mr Beaumont's mines.

Space fails me to tell about the storehouses, saw mills, ford, powder magazine, the library and reading room, and other appliances. Some notion may be formed of the magnitude of the operations from the fact that, including Allenheads and the mines of the West Allen, and in Weardale, 1400 dozen pounds of candles are burnt every month. But so far as it can be described in a few lines, I must say something about the wonderful economy of water power. From the reservoir in the hillside, 180 feet above Allenheads, the water descends, impels the two hydraulic engines, does all the work on the washing floors, drives the lathes, the saws, the machinery in the workshop, keeps four wheels going deep underground which pump water from the deepest levels of the mine, then escaping by an adit, it flows into the Allen about a mile to the north. Not long, however, does it run at liberty for, intercepted by a race, it flows along that for two miles to Brecon Hill - the first shaft on the Blackett level - there turns two wheels that force water into the accumulator and is discharged again into the Allen. Three-eighths of a mile farther it follows another race, works a corn mill and falls once more into the Allen. Then another race to Sipton - the second shaft on the Blackett level - then two more wheels and an accumulator, from which it has a quarter of a mile to itself in the Allen. Then another race, another corn mill, and yet another race to Holmes Lynn where it will have to drive three large wheels and perhaps supply a washing floor. Once more it falls into the Allen, flows two miles, turns another corn mill from which it runs half a mile under ground to work the great wheel of the Allen smelt-mill. After that it runs freely in its own channel. And besides all this, the Allen carries away all the refuse cast into it at Allenheads.

In the afternoon of my third day, I walked down the course of the Allen and along the new Blackett level, in company with Mr Bewick. This level is to be driven seven miles underground, running north and south, to explore for lead veins which run east and west; and it is a noteworthy example of mining enterprise. It is for the drainage of this level that the three high pressure hydraulic engines, with their tall accumulators are erected on the three sites already named. The walk was a clear case of the pursuit of knowledge under difficulties, so miry was the ground.

Allenheads Primitive Methodist Sunday School

The following extracts come from the log books of the Sunday School:

In 1859

There were 25 teachers and 102 scholars (60 boys and 42 girls) attending the Primitive Methodist Sunday School.

In 1928

There were 8 teachers and 40 scholars (17 boys and 23 girls) attending the Wesleyan Sunday School.

In 1943

There were 9 teachers and 59 scholars attending Sunday School in wartime when the Sunday Schools were joined together.

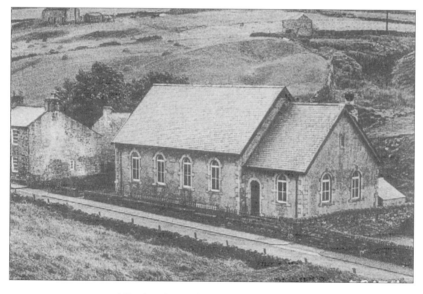

Allenheads Methodist Chapel c.1910

Henry French and Sarah Ridley in China

Henry (Harry) French Ridley spent around 40 years working as a Missionary in China. He married Sarah in 1894. On his return to England in 1932, now widowed, he came to Allenheads as a teacher at Allenheads Sunday School. He boarded with Mrs Pickering, infant teacher at Allenheads School.

1890   Henry French Ridley and Sarah Querry sail to China. He had previously been running a YMCA in Wakefield, she had been a parlourmaid in Brighton. They are married in 1894, and sent to Sining.

1895   July The Mahommedan Rebellion. A boy of 13 who survived the slaughter in Shih kia li is employed to look after Dora May, their eldest child.

1895   Oct/Nov Sining siege and civil war. "We have had more than 500 wounded patients ... nearly 1,000 diptheria patients ... we have been without lancets to cut out bullets but managed fairly well with a pocket knife."

1896   July 31, birth of John Edward, second and only other surviving child.

1904   John and Dora Ridley are sent to the missionary school at Chefoo. The school was founded in 1880 and in 1905 it had three buildings where it accommodated 100 boys and 50 girls as boarders, and where public exams were taken every other year. There was a preparatory school for 60 boarders. There were places for children of missionaries and merchants of good standing, but no Chinese or Eurasians. It was non-sectarian. There were holidays in August, December and January when most children went home. It was not easy to find teachers, especially for boys, as most of the 800 CIM members wanted to preach not teach.

1908   Henry and Sarah Ridley see their children at Chefoo for the first time in four years.

1909   HFR visits the Dalai Lama for the second time and presents him with bound copies of the Gospels in Tibetan.

1909   HFR visits Kumbum, Tankori, Tatung. "During the year we have dispensed medicines to over 2,000 patients."

1912   Mr and Mrs Ridley return to China from England via Siberia, leaving Dora and John to be further educated.

1913   Aug 23 Mrs Sarah Ridley dies in Kansu from typhus fever.

1916   A temporary church is built at Heo Tsi Ho by HFR, described as a church elder. "A high day in my missionary career, as it is our first out-station."

1918   The first Moslem convert.

1926   HFR plans to visit Tihwafu and Lanchowfu, a 54 day journey, to relieve a fellow missionary on furlough. He says he has walked up to 33 miles in a day - "not so bad for a man over 60".

1926   April 16 Lanchowfu "held up here, owing to the commandeering of every animal and cart the military can lay their hands on ... Over 3,000 soldiers have been baptised."

1930   Jan. Travels in Western China some nine months in duration are described as "dangerous journeys by intrepid pioneers".

1932   Leaving next Spring via Siberia.

Henry French Ridley 1923

Extracts from Log Books for Allenheads School

collected by Mrs Joan Ridley (née Philipson) of Ropehaugh

Sept 1 1906   J N Temperley
                      Correspondent

School built in 1848 by J W Beaumont Esq, his agents and workmen. It became a Board School in 1878 and a Council school in 1903. Headmaster Mr Craig.

Part of Report made by HMI Mr Brutflower after a visit on Sept 26 1907.

Attention improved but discipline weak. Children prompt each other and some eat in class. Until such practices are stopped satisfactory work can hardly be expected.

Arithmetic weak - the teaching too mechanical.

Reading lacks expression. No general reading book for the whole of standards 4-7 except an edition of Robinson Crusoe which has been in use for some time.

Since the last report a new infants teacher, Mrs Pickering, has been appointed and the order in this class is good and the work promises fairly well.

1907

Nov 15   Work is being pushed on vigorously. Attendance good and a parcel of exercise books proving useful.

Nov 26   Very cold. Snow has been falling and drifting since 10am.

1908

Jan 22   Sarah Hannah Longstaff a Std 1 girl died this morning from the effects of burns received at her home on Monday evening by her clothing catching fire from a lighted candle.

Feb 18   Mr Houldershaw of Newcastle gave a Temperance Lecture to the children this afternoon from 1-30 to 2-10.

Feb 20   Major Ramsey visited the school at 10am and saw the children drill and took them in drill himself.

March 2   Snow fell heavily over the weekend. Deep drifts. Only 15 children at school.

March 11   Roads being in a better state school was re-opened with 41 present. A path has been cut down the hill to the main road.

March 23   Mrs Pickering is absent owing to an attack of influenza. A number of children also ill.

March 26   Mrs Craig has taken duty for Mrs Pickering but now she has 'flu'. Miss Shield has kindly come to do Mrs Pickering's work.

April 10   Mr Ridley who was interred on Wednesday was in former years manager of this school and chairman of the Allendale School Board and mining agent at Allenheads for many years.

1909
June 9   School bell fell off while being rung. No one hurt, heavy bell.
Oct 4   George Lindsay commenced duty as Headmaster and found the school clock and bell in a state of disrepair.
Nov 2   A tea was given to the infants through the kindness of Mrs Pickering prior to the departure of John Edward Craig to the Sydenham Orphanage.

1913
Nov 14   Alfred Liddle received 4 strokes after ill-using Gertrude Vickers, her mother having complained.

1914
March 30   The following have received 2 strokes for absenting themselves on Friday afternoon last J William Ridley Elizabeth H Ridley Elizabeth Bright Thomas Nixon Joseph Parker Thomas Parker and Sarah Parker.

1915

Feb 22   Satchels of scent and flags have been sold by the children making 10/6d for comfort for soldiers.

March 15   Two Belgian children admitted today.

Aug 16   Nine boys absent to go beating. Gamekeeper sent note asking for 3 of these to be released. I advised him to apply to the manager.

1916

Sept 6   John Walker employed by J S Shield Junior to drive the post. This has gone on for some time.

Aug 28   Mary A Armstrong died from meningitis.

1918

Jan 11   Coldest week on record (one of). School taps frozen all week.

Jan 28   George Nixon back to school after being absent 3 days. He told me he had had "bad neck" yet he was helping in Co-op on Friday.

March 6   George Nixon and Eddie Charlton taking cow to Catton for J S Shield of the Inn. George's father not aware of the fact.

Nov 5   Instructed (managers) to close school till further notice because of the serious outbreak of influenza.

1919

Sept 26   R Heslop commenced school at Hexham after winning a scholarship.

Aug 17   One by one pupils are absent for haymaking.

1922

Feb 28   School closed for Princess Mary's wedding.

1924

Apr 9   School piano arrived.

June 21   School excursion to Silloth - 26 present scholars, 8 old scholars plus parents and friends went by charabanc calling at Naworth Castle and Carlisle.

July 16   Lord Allendale sent £10 towards the subscription list to send the children to Wembley.

Aug 25   Ada Chambers, Janet Philipson, Isabel Ridley, Maurice and Lesley Fairlamb absent visiting Wembley.

Aug 29   Lord and Lady Allendale entertained the children at the Hall and gave them all a present.

Sept 18   School closed for Burnfoot Show. Five first prizes and 4 second prizes won by the children.

1925

The children are on excellent terms with their mistress and work has improved. Infant division satisfactory.

March   School Concert. Operetto "The Fairy Chain" given by the scholars.
20-21   £10-15-0 was realized. Supper given by parents and friends.
March 27   School closed for children to attend Tynedale Musical Festival. Won Mrs
           Blackett Ord's Trophy to be held for 1 yr for the Extra Class for small
           schools. Won first also in the Novice Class. Children did remarkably well
           in the sight tests gaining highest marks.
April 9   £4 sent to the Lord Mayor of Newcastle as a donation to the Scotswood
           disaster relief fund. The children voluntarily without exception voted to
           give up their proposed excursion to the seaside so that the money could
           be used this way.
Dec 22   Severe snowstorm, only 7 children at school.

1926

Feb 19-20 Children performed Briar Rose before large audiences both evenings.

Feb 23   Children travelled by charabanc to Haltwhistle to give concert.
Feb 27   Children went to Rookhope to give concert.
June 5   School excursion to Keswick via Penrith. Lodore Falls visited by motor
           boat.
July 3   Children gave a display of country dancing at a Garden Fete held in Lord
           Allendale's grounds.

1927

March 5   Jennie Armstrong Middlehope and Mabel Philipson Ropehaugh have
           been certified medically unfit to attend school for 3 months (Dr Fletcher).
June 11   School excursion to Brampton..

1928

Jan 8   Owing to influenza epidemic the % of the school attendance has dropped
           to 43%.
July 3   Ruth Nixon contracted scarlet fever - taken to hospital.
July 4   Ruth Nixon died in hospital.
Sept 13   Iris Shield fractured her arm during this afternoon's interval and the
           accident has been reported to Mr Metcalfe (local manager).

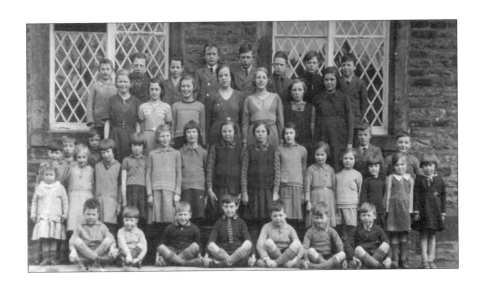

Allenheads School c.1935

Back row (left to right) - ? Makepeace, Ernest Dickinson, Donald Walker, Alan Johnson, Milton Sanderson, Jimmy Nixon, Eddie Blackstock, Billy Renwick.

2nd back row – Jimmy Dickinson, ? Makepeace, Lloyd Ridley, Iris Shield, Peggy Sanderson, Violet Hutchinson, Yvonne Halley, Joan Reynolds, Eva Nixon, Nancy Dickinson, Stephen Roddam, Norman ?.

2nd front row – Sylvia Makepeace, Maura Makepeace, Mary Kirkup, Reta Nixon, Beatty Sanderson, Edith Dodd, Hilda Nixon, Irene Nixon, Nancy Milburn, Kitty MacGregor, Vida Walker, Maud Sanderson, Joan Philipson, Sylvia Hewit.

Front row – Alan Dickinson, Reggie Sanderson, Jonny Kirkup, Dennis Sanderson, Raymond Walker, John Shield, Eric Sanderson.

<u>1929</u>

Aug 29   Miss Keenleyside was presented with a dinner service from the scholars and friends on the occasion of her leaving this school to take up duties at Newham.

Sept 2   Miss Pearson took up duties.

Dec 6   Epidemic of chicken pox.

<u>1931</u>

Feb 12   Epidemic of measles.

June 17   Mr Nuttall visited school today and examined Scripture.

<u>1932</u>

Jan   Attendance poor because of whooping cough.

Feb   Heavy snowstorms.

March 1   J A Kent begins duties as Headmistress today.

May 30   Nancy Milburn and Evelyn Hutchinson have attended Shaftoe Trust School for the purpose of having their eyes tested.

July 15   Evelyn Hutchinson leaves school, age 14.

Aug 29   Admitted Eric Sanderson to school (41 on books).

Dec 13   Removed William Dodd's name from register as he is nearly 15 and illness prevents his coming.

Dec 23   Closing for Christmas. Each child received an apple and orange from the teacher and a helping of Christmas pudding from Mrs Kent.

<u>1933</u>

Jan 9   School gates have been repaired by Mr Dodd (local blacksmith).

Feb 24   Poor attendance - severe snowstorm.

-March 6

April 19   School social Beaumont Hall. Proceeds £2-15-2.

May 1   Admitted Kitty McGregor.

May 2   Grading exam held in this school supervised by Miss Ferral (Keenley School) and Miss Pickering. Miss Kent took charge of St Peter's School.

May 10   Chester and Wesley Armstrong names removed from roll as they are moving to a farm at Sinderhope (38 on roll).

May 15   Audrey Dixon left school, moved to Allendale.

May 19   100% attendance in the upper school - first time since Miss Kent came and a while before - so pupils rewarded by a slightly early dismissal.

Dec 22   Fred Hutchinson left school (W.I. give children a party).

1934

Mar 29   Rene Vickers leaves school (14 yrs)

June 14   A party of 14 children and the teacher (JK) climbed Killhope Law.

June 8   43 pupils 21 parents and friends of the teachers went to W.Bay for Annual outing.

Aug 27   Admitted Joan Philipson to school. 47 on register. Matilda Roddam won 1st prize at the local show for map drawing.

1935

    M S (Sylvia) Hewitson admitted to school.

Jan 21   School milk (under government scheme) supplied today.

Feb 8   Matilda Roddam left school.

March 15   Helen Whitfield left school moved to Whitfield.

April 18   Iris Shield and Joan Reynolds left school.

May 6   School closed for Royal Jubilee Celebrations.

May 7   Allenheads St Peter's and Sinderhope joined for celebrations at St Peter's. Ideal weather conditions. Spent happy day. Children received mugs and sixpences, an orange and sweets, presented by R Hepple.

July 26   Alan Johnson left school.

Sept 30   Nancy Milburn won 2nd prize at the Agricultural Show for an essay "A great character in History" - Violet Hutchinson won 2nd prize for a knitted garment.

Nov 11   Report from HM Inspector
Both teachers very satisfactory. Children well-mannered and friendly. It is clear they are under good influence. Work in good order but tone of the singing unnecessarily harsh.

Nov 25   Stephen and Cyril Roddam moved to St John's Chapel and Kitty MacGregor to Scotland.

Nov 28   Amount realized by sale of poppies in the area including the school £2-6-9.

Dec 20   Milton Sanderson leaves school.

1936

Jan 10   Dr Fletcher visited school to immunize children against diphtheria (epidemic at Allendale).

Jan 20   Mr J W Metcalfe died, Estate Agent for Viscount Allendale and a manager of this school for 20 yrs.

April 28   Edward Blackstock sat the Naval Scholarship Exam under my supervision.

Sept 22   A bus load of scholars parents and teachers went to St John's Chapel to see a circus. Many children had never seen a circus before.

Nov 9   E Blackstock left school going to work in mines at Sparty Lea.

Dec 22   J Kent appointment terminates today. Take up duties at Ashington.

1937
Jan   Margaret E Fields temporary teacher.
March 18 Alan Foster Nancy Dickinson and Eva Nixon left.

1938
April   J A Younger began duties.
Sept 30   Mrs Pickering leaves school today, retiring as infant teacher since 26/8/1907. Scholars past and present gave her an armchair.
Oct 14   John Shield and Eric Sanderson given permission to attend a stock sale in connection with YFC (calf club).
Nov 12   Miss J Robertson infants teacher.

1939
April 6   B Sanderson and Dennis Short left school. Now 21 on register.
June 1   Roland Armstrong admitted to school.
June 26   Clifford Dodd admitted to school.
July 21   Miss Robertson leaves school.
Sept 1   School closed for reception of evacuees.
Sept 14   School re-opened today. Now 46 pupils including evacuees.

1940
March   Children gave concert for W.I. comforts fund for the troops and raised £5-17-9.

1941
Jan 20   School closed because of severe snowstorm.
Feb 17   Snowstorm again. Drifts 3-6 feet on school bank.
June   Miss Mary Dormand new infant teacher.

1943
May 31   Miss Younger, now Mrs Harrison, leaves school today.
June 1   Miss Cuthbert new Headmistress.
Nov 8   Edwin Batchelor granted 20 extra clothing coupons (growing fast).

Elizabeth Sanderson, quilter

Elizabeth Sanderson, 1861-1933, outside her home and workshop at Fawside Green, Allenheads with two of her apprentices (Jennifer Peart is standing in doorway) c.1910. Elizabeth had been an apprentice of George Gardner, a quilter and draper of Smelt Mill Cottages. She was a highly successful and influential quilter and designer.

One of her distinctive and original designs - the "Sanderson Star".

Robert Ridley's spar box

The illuminated interior of Robert Ridley's spar box on display
at Killhope, the North of England Lead Mining Museum.

Robert Ridley, 1867-1929, was a lead miner like his father before him. He was a devout Methodist and lay preacher and lived at Chapel Cottages, Allenheads, with his wife Mary Jane and family. Like many miners he collected spar crystals. By the second half of the 19th century spar boxes were built for public display as well as for decoration. Robert 's spar box attracted great admiration when it was exhibited in 1896 at local fairs and shows. The superbly crafted mahogany display cabinet with interior of illuminated display of spar and mineral crystals are displayed at Killhope.

Mr & Mrs W. Ridley, Edna and friend beside their stack of peats on Whetstone Mea.

Allenheads Women's Bright Hour outing:
Mrs Ada Philipson, Mrs Brown, Mrs M.A. Ridley, Miss Kirkby,
Miss E. Wood, Mrs Edith Robson & Mrs Minnie Hewitson.

Tom Milburn, Jim Teasdale & Matt Varty stonewalling c.1940

Fred Hutchinson & Dennis Short

Acknowledgements

Without the generous offer from Fiona Hewitt to retype the original text, this new book would not have been possible and I am most grateful to her.

My thanks also to Hilary Kristensen of Wagtail Press for agreeing to publish "Sparty Lea" again and to Tom Kristensen for his design expertise. I am much indebted to Ann Rooke for producing the detailed map of Sparty Lea on the inside front cover.

My most grateful thanks are offered to the following people for their kindness in loaning me material, for their permission in allowing me to use information and for their help towards the compilation of this book: Willie Parker, without whose memory, conversation and never failing help this book would never have been started and certainly never completed, Joe Sparke, Joan Ridley, Joyce Short, Derek & Edward Varty, John Coulson, Elsom Robson, Irene Owen, Annie Featherstone, Herbert & Lucy Robson, Dorothy Baitey, Willie Hudspith, John Osborne, Louis Robson, Lawrence Graham, Thomas M. Bell jnr., Mrs T.M. Bell, Monica Sanderson, Elinor Sanderson, Ian Forbes of Killhope Lead Mining Museum, Vicki Feaver, Raymond Archer, Jo Hutton, The Newcastle Chronicle, Hexham Courant and The Northern Echo. My thanks to them all.

List of Illustrations